Presented to

_____

By

_____

On the Occasion of

_____

Date

_____

365
ONE-MINUTE MEDITATIONS

WONDERFUL NAMES OF OUR WONDERFUL LORD

FROM THE POPULAR DAILY DEVOTIONAL

HURLBURT & HORTON

365

ONE-MINUTE MEDITATIONS

WONDERFUL NAMES OF OUR WONDERFUL LORD

FROM THE POPULAR DAILY DEVOTIONAL

HURLBURT & HORTON

BARBOUR

PUBLISHING

Printed in India.

A Minute a Day Can Change Your Life

We're all busy and pressed for time. But somewhere in our daily schedule, there must be at least sixty free seconds. Look for that open minute and fill it with this book. *365 One-Minute Meditations: Wonderful Names of Our Wonderful Lord* provides a quick but powerful reading for every day of the year, promising real spiritual impact. Each day's entry features a carefully selected verse from God's Word, along with a condensed reading from *Wonderful Names of Our Wonderful Lord*, the popular daily devotional featuring 365 names and titles of Jesus Christ from both the Old and New Testaments.

First published in 2005, *Wonderful Names of Our Wonderful Lord* has continued to help readers understand the multifaceted character of the Alpha and Omega.

If you're seeking a spiritual lift, try *365 One-Minute Meditations: Wonderful Names of Our Wonderful Lord*. You'll only need a minute a day—but the benefits could be life-changing.

THE SEED OF THE WOMAN

*And I will put enmity between thee and the woman,
and between thy seed and her seed.*
GENESIS 3:15

Our Savior came from the bosom of the Father
to become the "Seed of the Woman." He turned
from "the word that I have spoken, the same
shall judge [you]" (John 12:48), to be in His
innocence judged of sinful men and crucified.
O Jesus, we bow before Thee in worship and
adoration.

THE ANGEL OF JEHOVAH

And the angel of the LORD called unto
Abraham out of heaven the second time.
GENESIS 22:15

The Angel (or Messenger) of Jehovah was
Himself God's message to us. O Thou who dost
Thyself bring Thine own message to heal our
deep desolations—Thou art our sin offering.
We praise Thee for the glory which Thou givest
in our pain by Thine own radiant presence and
worship Thee, O "Angel of Jehovah."

Shiloh (Peacemaker)

The sceptre shall not depart from Judah, nor a lawgiver from between his feet, until Shiloh come; and unto him shall the gathering of the people be.

Genesis 49:10

Israel must walk in darkness under law, but "Shiloh" comes at last and peace. Has Shiloh come to thee? Has the peace which passeth understanding entered into thy soul? For Shiloh conquered every foe that could harass thee, and stands today offering peace.

THE STONE OF ISRAEL

His bow abode in strength, and the arms of his hands were made strong by the hands of the mighty God of Jacob; (from thence is the shepherd, the stone of Israel).
GENESIS 49:24

O Chief Cornerstone, make me a polished, living stone, always a part of Thy temple. Holy Lord, self-offered for my peace; through death that I might live, through fire that I might become indestructible—enlighten me today.

MANNA

*And the house of Israel called
the name thereof Manna.*
EXODUS 16:31

An exhausted life may gather new strength for
an onward march. The Master feeds the souls
of His children Himself—a spiritual "Manna."
To "feed upon the Lord" may sound like empty
mysticism but may be a fact to every trusting
soul. For unto us are given "exceeding great and
precious promises: that by these ye might be
partakers of the divine nature" (2 Peter 1:4).

THE MEAT (MEAL) OFFERING

*When any will offer a meat offering unto the LORD,
his offering shall be of fine flour; and he shall pour
oil upon it, and put frankincense thereon.*

LEVITICUS 2:1

Most Holy Meal Offering, as Thou didst pour
upon the fine meal of Thy perfect life the Holy
Oil of Thy Holy Spirit, and the frankincense of
Thy perfect adoration, and offer all for me, so I
pour forth my soul in worship.

THE PEACE OFFERING

And if his oblation be a sacrifice of peace offering. . .
he shall offer it without blemish before the LORD.
LEVITICUS 3:1

Is there any point of dispute between thy Lord
and thee? One little thing which thou dost not
surrender? He has made the offering which
atones for all thy past, but thou must yield thy
will to Him. Shall it be now?

8

JANUARY

A STAR

I shall see him, but not now: I shall behold him,
but not nigh: there shall come a Star out of Jacob.

NUMBERS 24:17

What could be more fitting than that our
Lord should be called of God a "Star"? From
far beyond our world of trouble and care and
change, He shines with undimmed light, a
radiant, guiding Star to all who will follow Him.

A SCEPTER

A Sceptre shall rise out of Israel.
NUMBERS 24:17

Someday all the world shall know that a "Scepter" shall rise out of Israel, and evil will be destroyed before His righteousness. It is in the very nature of things that sin must be consumed before His glorious holiness. Can it be other than the love of sin that blinds the eyes of men to His consuming righteousness?

10
JANUARY

THE CAPTAIN OF
THE HOST OF THE LORD

*As captain of the host
of the LORD am I now come.*
JOSHUA 5:14

Captain of the hosts of God,
In the path where Thou hast trod,
Bows my soul in humble awe—
Take command. Thy word is law.
Cause me to possess the land,
Led by Thine almighty hand.
Be my guide, defense, and power;
Lead me from this very hour.

THE ROCK OF MY SALVATION

The LORD liveth; and blessed be my rock;
and exalted be the God of the rock of my salvation.
2 SAMUEL 22:47

No graver danger threatens the believer than
that of forgetting that he was redeemed. To
meet this need, our Savior pictures Himself as
the "Rock of our Salvation." Let us glory in this
precious name and never forget that He was
"wounded for our transgressions" (Isaiah 53:5).

THE LIGHT OF THE MORNING

*He shall be as the light of the morning, when
the sun riseth, even a morning without clouds.*
2 SAMUEL 23:4

When the great glory of that morning of our
eternal life in heaven shall break upon us, we
shall find that He who lighted all our earthly
pilgrimage is still our source of life over there
and will be to those for whom He has prepared
a place, the "Light of the Morning."

TENDER GRASS

*And he shall be. . .as the tender grass springing
out of the earth by clear shining after rain.*
2 SAMUEL 23:4

The Good Shepherd leads His flock in
pastures where the tender grass brings to
them all-sufficient nourishment as they feed
on Him. Open now the Book of books
and feed on Him who is the Living Word,
the "Tender Grass," which satisfies and
builds up His hungry sheep.

THE DAYSMAN

Neither is there any daysman betwixt us,
that might lay his hand upon us both.
JOB 9:33

When the day of reckoning comes, when I shall
stand before the Father, stripped of all pretense
and shame, then will I fear no evil, for my
"Daysman," Mediator, Arbitrator, will stand
and speak for me. Can I do less than bow upon
my face and worship Him now and throughout
eternity?

MY GLORY

But thou, O LORD, art a shield for me;
my glory, and the lifter up of mine head.
PSALM 3:3

That God is "glory"—or "excellence"—beyond our understanding, none can deny. But do our hearts look up to Him today in worship and speak the truth—"Thou art my Glory"? Our deepest, holiest joy comes only when we humbly say in the hour of secret worship, "Thou art mine."

THE LIFTER UP OF MINE HEAD

But thou, O LORD, art a shield for me; my glory,
and the lifter up of mine head.
PSALM 3:3

O Thou who hast given
Thy glory to me,
Anoint my blind eyes
Till Thy glory I see.

Lift up my bowed head,
Be my shield and my light,
Till Thy radiant glory
Shall banish my night.

FORTRESS

*The LORD is my rock, and my fortress, and my deliverer;
my God, my strength, in whom I will trust; my buckler,
and the horn of my salvation, and my high tower.*

PSALM 18:2

"A mighty fortress is my God," and no evil may
reach the soul that shelters there. Every failure
of our lives and each defeat has come when we
have sought some earthly fortress rather than
our Lord.

A WORM AND NO MAN

*But I am a worm, and no man; a reproach of men,
and despised of the people.*
PSALM 22:6

Few harder experiences come to God's children
than when those who should be friendly
unjustly make us a reproach. Yet He has walked
that way before us. He, too, was a "Reproach of
Men"! Shall not the servant walk there, too, and
be like Him who in such suffering "opened not
His mouth" (Isaiah 53:7)?

MY SHEPHERD

The LORD is my shepherd;
I shall not want.
PSALM 23:1

To say, "The Lord is my Shepherd," must carry
with it in our understanding not merely grateful
praise for the infinite grace and tenderness of
the Great Shepherd who leads us by still waters
and in green pastures, but confession of our
own helplessness and need of a Shepherd's care.
And a remembrance also of our lost, undone
condition.

20

JANUARY

RESTORER

He restoreth my soul: he leadeth me in the
paths of righteousness for his name's sake.
PSALM 23:3

We wander from God and from the paths of
righteousness—from following Him beside
the still waters—till we lose the way, lose joy,
lose the sound of His voice. Then the Master
"restoreth our soul"—brings us back into His
way, into the paths of righteousness.

THE STRONG
AND MIGHTY JEHOVAH

Who is the King of glory? Jehovah strong and mighty.
PSALM 24:8 ASV

Is thy heart faint? Thy strength but utter
weakness? Behold thy Lord—Jehovah—He
who reveals Himself as "Strong and Mighty"—a
soldier, a warrior, with sufficient power to break
down every opposition. Strong and Mighty
Jehovah, give me victory over all the power of
the enemy this day.

JEHOVAH, MIGHTY IN BATTLE

*Who is the King of glory? . . .
Jehovah mighty in battle.*
PSALM 24:8 ASV

No life can be lived for God in these difficult days without terrific conflict. Principalities and powers are arrayed against the child of God who seeks to serve his Master. We have no might with which to meet this great host that cometh out against us, but "Jehovah, Mighty in Battle," is our Savior, our Intercessor, our ever-present Friend.

KING OF GLORY

Who is this King of glory?
The LORD of hosts, he is the King of glory.
PSALM 24:10

Jehovah Jesus, the glorious King! Not merely a king, but glorious, excelling all others in mighty truth and power, grace and love. We almost forget for a time His absolute sovereignty as we bow in humble worship before His matchless glory and cry again and again, "Thy kingdom come, O glorious King."

MY STRONG ROCK

Bow down thine ear to me; deliver me speedily:
be thou my strong rock, for an house of defence to save me.
PSALM 31:2

No sorrow of men is so deep as to be without
a refuge. The Man of Sorrows bore thy sin in
His own body. He carried all thy grief. He is thy
"Strong Rock." A strong, safe house, in which
thou art defended from thyself, the world,
the devil.

MY ROCK AND MY FORTRESS

For thou art my rock and my fortress;
therefore for thy name's sake lead me, and guide me.
PSALM 31:3

Are we built upon that High Rock which is a Fortress so that we shall stand secure? Lord Jesus, may we seek to gather "gold and silver and precious stones," that we may bring some honor to Thee by building that which shall endure through all the ages.

A STRONG TOWER

*For thou hast been a shelter for me,
and a strong tower from the enemy.*
PSALM 61:3

Did ever a child of God in danger hasten within the "Strong Tower" of His presence and find aught of failure or defeat? Must we not confess that every failure has come when we were found outside? O Thou Strong Tower, may we enter in today and dwell in Thee and be safe.

THE ROCK THAT IS HIGHER THAN I

*From the end of the earth will I cry unto thee,
when my heart is overwhelmed: lead me
to the rock that is higher than I.*
PSALM 61:2

Not down to a dungeon deep,
Nor to level of earth, hard by—
But lead, when the storm o'erwhelms,
To the "Rock That Is Higher Than I."

There will I worship and wait,
Redeemed with the saints on high.
All glory and honor and praise
To the "Rock That Is Higher Than I."

A STRANGER AND AN ALIEN

I am become a stranger unto my brethren,
and an alien unto my mother's children.
PSALM 69:8

What was the price He paid,
That, what He bore for me;
"A Stranger, an Alien"; alone,
He died on Calvary.

A "Stranger" to make me a friend,
An "Alien" to give me a home.
Great Stranger, I fall at Thy feet;
No longer from Thee will I roam.

THE KING'S SON

*Give the king thy judgments, O God,
and thy righteousness unto the king's son.*
PSALM 72:1

How little do our hearts discern the homage due
to God as King and to Jesus as His Son. Do we,
as we enter the house of God, bow humbly and
revere the "King's Son"? Do wandering thoughts
of earthly things deprive us of the blessing and
the answer to our prayers?

RAIN UPON MOWN GRASS

*He shall come down like rain
upon the mown grass.*
PSALM 72:6

My soul was parched with the fire of sin,
My life mowed down with pain,
My Savior spoke, "My child, draw near."
His word was like the rain.

Refreshing, cleansing, lifting me,
My Lord, my All, came down,
And now I turn from all earth's dross—
To gain a heavenly crown.

SHOWERS THAT WATER THE EARTH

He shall come down like rain upon the mown grass:
as showers that water the earth.
PSALM 72:6

Our lives grow dusty, dry, and desert in our earthly pilgrimage, but He who seeks a love that is fresh and pure and strong comes down upon us as the "Showers That Water the Earth." Have you turned to Him today and found that cool, refreshing, cleansing blessing which He seeks to give?

My Firstborn

Also I will make him my firstborn,
higher than the kings of the earth.
Psalm 89:27

The Eternal Father, God, is speaking. "My Firstborn I will make higher than the kings of earth." O thou who art the last-born of the Father, the Firstborn is thy Elder Brother. Thou hast shared His humiliation to thy salvation. Thou shalt share His exaltation to thine eternal glory. We worship Thee, Lord Jesus, God's "Firstborn"!

THE HEAD STONE OF THE CORNER

*The stone which the builders refused is
become the head stone of the corner.*
PSALM 118:22

God has laid aside all human plans and made
our Lord and Savior the "Head Stone of the
Corner." When all human buildings crumble
and every man-taught architect has failed, all
hearts bow before that perfect building, that
eternal temple, worshipping Him who is its
crown of grace.

FEBRUARY

MY HIGH TOWER

My fortress; my high tower, and my deliverer;
my shield, and he in whom I trust;
who subdueth my people under me.
PSALM 144:2

"My High Tower" is a vision of our glorious Savior as the Most High—high above our trials; high above our temptations; high above our foes; high above our failures and losses; high above the care of our earthward life. A place of holy calm and peace and stillness.

EXCELLENT

Let them praise the name of the LORD:
for his name alone is excellent.
PSALM 148:13

All the glory of the Lord is that in which He
excels all others. His name is "Excellent," and all
His names which represent some feature of His
grace are glorious because they excel any other
name ever uttered among men. What friend,
what helper do we know on earth who ever has
or can approach His excellence?

WISDOM

*I wisdom dwell with prudence,
and find out knowledge of witty inventions.*
PROVERBS 8:12

Wisdom is the right use of knowledge. What a wondrous name for Him who gave Himself for us! Who, "when He putteth forth His own sheep, . . .goeth before them" (John 10:4); who guides us by the skillfulness of His hand. May we seek with all our hearts until we find Thee, and finding Thee, find Wisdom to do the will of God.

UNDERSTANDING

Counsel is mine, and sound wisdom:
I am understanding; I have strength.
PROVERBS 8:14

God is Love, God is Light, God is to us
a thousand things for which we long and
which we need; but have we realized that in
possessing Him and abiding in Him, He is
"Understanding" and all that seems dark and
difficult will become clear to us as we depend
upon Him?

A Friend That Sticketh Closer Than a Brother

A man that hath friends must shew himself friendly:
and there is a friend that sticketh closer than a brother.
Proverbs 18:24

"There is a Friend," though all the world deny
it. One who is always true and faithful. One
who never leaves and never forsakes. No brother
can abide as He. Wilt thou be friend to Jesus, as
He is friend to thee?

Ointment Poured Forth

Because of the savour of thy good ointments
thy name is as ointment poured forth.
Song of Solomon 1:3

Is thy soul sore from sin or from the fiery darts
of Satan, of sinners, or of saints? Then is thy
Lord to thee as "Ointment Poured Forth," free,
abundant, ready, healing, and fragrant. Come
near to Him and let that healing Ointment pour
over thee and soothe and heal thee.

A BUNDLE OF MYRRH

A bundle of myrrh is my well-beloved unto me.
SONG OF SOLOMON 1:13

A missionary, wearily walking a winding
pathway in the night, suddenly came upon a
spot where the air was heavy with the perfume
of wild jasmine and was comforted and
refreshed by a fragrance preserved from wild
animals for a sorrowing toiler. So is thy Lord, to
thee, a "Bundle of Myrrh."

A Cluster of Camphire

*My beloved is unto me as a cluster of
camphire in the vineyards of Engedi.*
Song of Solomon 1:14

Struggling in the midst of experiences that
are not fragrant, that are not delightful, hast
thou learned to turn to Him who, in the
midst of darkness, is Light, in the midst of
unpleasantness is to thee exquisite delight?
Dost thou know thy Lord as a "Cluster of
Camphire"?

THE ROSE OF SHARON

I am the rose of Sharon.
SONG OF SOLOMON 2:1

There is no mood of thy life where Jesus fails to fit thy need; to brighten as a brilliant rose thy life. In joy or sorrow, sunshine or shadow, day or night, He blooms for thee. Behold Him, then, today, not only on the cross for thee, not only on the throne, but near thee, close beside thy path, the "Rose of Sharon."

THE LILY OF THE VALLEYS

I am. . .the lily of the valleys.
SONG OF SOLOMON 2:1

Sweetest, fairest, most exquisite flower that eye hath seen hidden save to eyes that seek it out. So does thy Lord unveil Himself to thee, even though thou walkest through the valleys. Only in those deeper shadows canst thou know His utter loveliness. Behold Him, then, and "fear no evil" (Psalm 23:4).

THE CHIEFEST AMONG TEN THOUSAND

My beloved is. . .the chiefest among ten thousand.
SONG OF SOLOMON 5:10

Is He really first in our hearts' affection? If so, His presence has been real to us. Here the secret of full transforming communion with our Lord Jesus Christ is found in gazing upon Him in all the beauty of His holiness, until in very truth He becomes in our hearts the "Chiefest among Ten Thousand."

HIM WHOM MY SOUL LOVETH

I will seek him whom my soul loveth.
SONG OF SOLOMON 3:2

Not in the doubting throng,
Not in the boastful song,
But kneeling—with Christ above me—
Humbly I'll say, "I love Thee."

Not with my lips alone,
Not for Thy gifts I own,
But just for the grace I see,
Jesus, my soul loveth Thee.

ALTOGETHER LOVELY

His mouth is most sweet: yea, he is altogether lovely.
SONG OF SOLOMON 5:16

Every earthly joy will pall,
Every earthly friend will fall.
Only Christ is to the end
"Altogether Lovely," friend.

Do you see His wondrous face?
Full of glory, love, and grace?
Look, and all thy need confess,
Worship His pure holiness.

THE BRANCH OF THE LORD

*In that day shall the branch of the LORD
be beautiful and glorious.*
ISAIAH 4:2

By every means and picture which we can
understand, the Spirit reveals our Savior's
oneness with God. None is more clear or full
of meaning to us than this, the "Branch of the
Lord." One with the Father, growing out of and
yet a part of Him. And we are "branches" of
Christ.

JEHOVAH OF HOSTS

One cried unto another, and said, Holy, holy, holy,
is Jehovah of hosts: the whole earth is full of his glory.
ISAIAH 6:3 ASV

If we always think of Jehovah as "God revealing
Himself," and the words of Jehovah-Jesus,
"Blessed are the pure in heart, for they shall see
God" (Matthew 5:8), then shall the heavens
about us be always full of the chariots and
horsemen of Jehovah of Hosts, and all fear shall
be stilled.

THE CHILD

For before the child shall know to refuse the evil,
and choose the good, the land that thou abhorrest
shall be forsaken of both her kings.
ISAIAH 7:16

The first, last, and chiefest mark of Christ's
deity was His great humility. The greatest Sage
and Seer of all the ages, a "Child"! Then shall we
hesitate to "become as little children" (Matthew
18:3), knowing that only so shall we enter the
kingdom?

A Sanctuary

And he shall be for a sanctuary.
ISAIAH 8:14

Where is thy place of worship? Where shall our souls find the place to pray? "He shall be for a Sanctuary," closer to thee than breathing, nearer than hands or feet. At any moment during all the hurried day, thou mayest be hidden from all earth's eyes, and still from all earth's din. Only abide in Him.

A Great Light

The people that walked in darkness have seen a great light: they that dwell in the land of the shadow of death, upon them hath the light shined.

ISAIAH 9:2

It is the people who once walked in darkness who are able to see the greatness of the light. Have you seen the Light? Lord, let my life and lips tell out the story of the Light my eyes have seen.

21
FEBRUARY

WONDERFUL

For unto us a child is born, unto us a son is given. . .
and his name shall be called Wonderful.
ISAIAH 9:6

Today Jesus is working just as wonderful
works as when He created the heaven and the
earth. His wondrous grace, His wonderful
omnipotence, is for His child who needs Him.
Attempt great things for God and expect great
things from Him, and you will begin to say,
"His name is Wonderful."

COUNSELOR

*For unto us a child is born, unto us a son is given. . .
and his name shall be called. . .Counsellor.*
ISAIAH 9:6

Not often is He called "Counselor" now. Even
God's saints continuously ask of men instead
of God, "How may I find God's will?" But
how rarely do we seek that heavenly wisdom,
that divine counsel, which alone will enable us
to find our way out of the mazes in which we
wander.

23
FEBRUARY

THE MIGHTY GOD

For unto us a child is born, unto us a son is given. . .
and his name shall be called. . .The mighty God.
ISAIAH 9:6

Have we doubted His might and feared in
the day when some foe was near? His name is
the "Mighty God." Then away with all doubt
and fear! Lord, I bow to the dust and worship.
Mighty God, show Thy power in me!

THE EVERLASTING FATHER

For unto us a child is born, unto us a son is given. . .
and his name shall be called. . .The everlasting Father.
ISAIAH 9:6

The Child who was born in Bethlehem, who
gave His life for thee, is not alone thy Savior
and king, but the "Everlasting Father." In His
everlasting love, within His everlasting arms,
within His Father-heart which pitieth thee—His
child—thou shalt find safety, rest, and comfort.

25

FEBRUARY

THE PRINCE OF PEACE

*For unto us a child is born, unto us a son is given. . .
and his name shall be called. . . The Prince of Peace.*
ISAIAH 9:6

He who proclaimed, "Peace I leave with you"
(John 14:27), is rightly called the "Prince of
Peace." He who brought such peace to earth
waits still to be crowned on earth; but He
gives before that royal day a peace that passeth
understanding to every trusting heart.

THE LIGHT OF ISRAEL

The light of Israel shall be for a fire, and his Holy One for a flame: and it shall burn and devour his thorns and his briers in one day.

ISAIAH 10:17

The "Light of Israel" was "to burn and devour thorns and briers." Are you bringing the unlovely things of your life into the light of His presence that they may be consumed? Shall we not ask Him to consume all evil in us?

A ROD OUT OF THE STEM OF JESSE

There shall come forth a rod out of the stem of Jesse.
ISAIAH 11:1

"Surely He hath borne our griefs" (Isaiah 53:4) and the way of our peace was in Him. Because He stooped so low God hath exalted Him very high, and the comeliness of a tender plant was the glory of God on high.

A Branch Out of His Roots

A Branch shall grow out of his roots.
ISAIAH 11:1

Out of the nations scattered over the earth, there came forth, as the prophet said, a "Branch Out of His Roots" of the stem of Jesse. And He who was of the seed of David shall just as surely come again to reign once more over Israel, and through Israel over all the earth.

I

MARCH

THE ROOT OF JESSE

In that day there shall be a root of Jesse. . .
to it shall the Gentiles seek: and his rest shall be glorious.
ISAIAH 11:10

All the gracious promises God gave to David
and his seed belong to us who worship Jesus.
How all the grace and glory of God through all
ages is gathered up for us who from the Gentile
world bow at His feet and find His glorious rest!

THE ENSIGN OF THE PEOPLE

*And in that day there shall be a root of Jesse,
which shall stand for an ensign of the people.*
ISAIAH 11:10

Jesus is the people's flag, an "Ensign of the
People." Wherever and whenever He is lifted
up, the people seek after Him. Is not our
failure to win many to the Lord due to our
misrepresentation of Him?

3
MARCH

MY STRENGTH AND MY SONG

God is my salvation; I will trust, and not be afraid:
for the LORD JEHOVAH is my strength and my song.
ISAIAH 12:2

We know Jehovah is our "Strength," but do
we make Him also our "Song"? We are able to
"trust and not be afraid" only as we sing of Him.
Our Redeemer is our "Strength." Let's make
Him our "Song" today.

A Nail Fastened in a Sure Place

I will fasten him as a nail in a sure place; and he shall be for a glorious throne to his father's house.

ISAIAH 22:23

A "Nail Fastened in a Sure Place" brings to the worshipping child of God a sense of the security of Christ in His relationship to the temple and throne of God.

5
MARCH

A Glorious Throne to His Father's House

And he shall be for a glorious
throne to his father's house.
Isaiah 22:23

Let it be no longer hard or difficult for thee to pray. The throne before which you bow is not one of austere justice but rather one of infinite grace. "Let us therefore come boldly unto the throne of grace, that we may obtain mercy, and find grace to help" (Hebrews 4:16).

STRENGTH TO THE POOR AND NEEDY

Thou hast been a strength to the poor,
a strength to the needy in his distress.
ISAIAH 25:4

Touched with the feeling of our infirmities, our Lord becomes a "Strength to the Poor and Needy." Let us never forget that His strength is made perfect in our weakness only when we realize our helplessness and fling ourselves into the outstretched arms by which He "created the heavens and the earth" (Genesis 1:1).

A SHADOW FROM THE HEAT

Thou hast been. . .a shadow from the heat.
ISAIAH 25:4

In the intolerable heat of the sun as it beats
upon equatorial Africa, one may step from the
unbearable heat to a shade so refreshing that it
is almost beyond belief. Thus our Lord pictures
Himself to His weary, toiling children as a
"Shadow from the Heat," into whose presence
we may step at any moment and find cool,
refreshing rest.

A REFUGE FROM THE STORM

Thou hast been. . .a refuge from the storm. . .
when the blast of the terrible ones
is as a storm against the wall.
ISAIAH 25:4

It needs must be that we pass through storms
and that we feel their force and chilling blast,
for only in such experiences could we ever know
the comfort of Him who is our "Refuge from
the Storm." Are we hiding in Him?

THE ROCK OF AGES

Trust ye in Jehovah for ever; for in Jehovah,
even Jehovah, is an everlasting rock.
ISAIAH 26:4 ASV

The strongest rocks in which men hide the
bodies of departed friends are ofttimes riven by
a growing plant. But He who calls us to "trust
in Jehovah forever" calls Himself an "Everlasting
Rock" or the "Rock of Ages." Let us trust in
Him today, tomorrow, and forever.

A CROWN OF GLORY

*In that day shall the LORD of hosts be for a crown
of glory. . .unto the residue of his people.*
ISAIAH 28:5

Thou who art redeemed from among the
lost, who wast dead and art alive, behold His
wondrous grace! The King of kings, the Lord of
lords, shall be to thee a "Crown of Glory." Then
fall at His feet today and worship Him with all
thy heart.

A Diadem of Beauty

In that day shall the LORD of hosts be for. . .
a diadem of beauty, unto the residue of his people.
ISAIAH 28:5

O humble child of God, behold the exceeding
grace which shall be revealed in the ages to
come. The beauty of the Lord our God shall be
upon thee, and He shall be to thee a crown or
"Diadem of Beauty."

The Foundation

*Therefore thus saith the Lord GOD, Behold,
I lay in Zion for a foundation a stone.*
ISAIAH 28:16

Of all the gracious promises concerning the
children of God, none is more wonderful than
that which describes the saints as polished stones
in the temple where He dwells. With divine
grace our Lord calls Himself the "Foundation,"
an "Everlasting Rock," the "Rock of Ages."
Where stands our faith today?

A SURE FOUNDATION

*Therefore thus saith the Lord GOD, Behold,
I lay in Zion. . .a sure foundation.*
ISAIAH 28:16

All the polishing of experiences through which
we pass is costly. Is it worthwhile? Worthwhile
to suffer on and say, "Dear Lord, stay not Thine
hand to comfort us and steady us." Through
just such testing times, the Master calls Himself
a "Sure Foundation." He who builds upon that
"Sure Foundation" finds his building sure.

A Tried Stone

Thus saith the Lord GOD, Behold,
I lay in Zion for a foundation a stone,
a tried stone, a precious corner stone.
ISAIAH 28:16

Surely the Father knew the Son. Yet He was tried of God that He might leave us an "example that [we] should follow His steps" (1 Peter 2:21). Let us bid the Master Builder to try us and chisel us until we fit in the place He has prepared for us.

**15
MARCH**

A Covert from
the Tempest

A man shall be as. . .a covert from the tempest.
ISAIAH 32:2

Of no other being could such language be used
as that used in the Word of God to picture
the grace and glory of our Lord. When the
destructive tempests sweep and we hide in Him,
shall we be safe? He shall be a "Covert from
the Tempest"—covered, sheltered, safe. Are we
hiding in Him?

**16
MARCH**

AS A HIDING PLACE
FROM THE WIND

A man shall be as an hiding place from the wind.
ISAIAH 32:2

The storms of hate, of evil, and of sin sweep
over our lives as we journey toward our
everlasting home. But for every soul who knows
his own helplessness, our Savior is Himself a
"Hiding Place from the Wind."

**17
MARCH**

SHADOW OF A GREAT ROCK IN A WEARY LAND

*A man shall be as. . .the shadow
of a great rock in a weary land.*
ISAIAH 32:2

O weary child, when thy strength fails and thou
canst go no further, sit down and lean back
in the shadow of thy Lord, upon Him. Build
there in prayer the fire of faith and find rest and
refreshment for thine onward march.

18
MARCH

As Rivers of Water in a Dry Place

A man shall be as. . .rivers of water in a dry place.
ISAIAH 32:2

To know the blessing of water in abundance, we need to have felt a very keen thirst. No matter how deep our thirst, how great our longing or our need, He who is as "Rivers of Water in a Dry Place" has said, "Lo, I am with you. Drink, and be satisfied."

THE KING IN HIS BEAUTY

Thine eyes shall see the king in his beauty:
they shall behold the land that is very far off.
ISAIAH 33:17

Do our lives see the "King in His Beauty"? O
Lord, let every mist and veil that hide Thy glory
be removed, and every sin be put away, that
we may behold Thee in the beauty of holiness.
Then the beauty of the Lord thy God shall be
upon us.

20
MARCH

OUR LAWGIVER

For the LORD is our judge, the LORD is our lawgiver,
the LORD is our king; he will save us.
ISAIAH 33:22

He who gave us life, He who has lived the life
we need to live—He knows. He made the law
for us in infinite tenderness and love. "He that
hath my commandments, and keepeth them, he
it is that loveth me" (John 14:21).

21
MARCH

JEHOVAH

The voice of one that crieth, Prepare ye in the
wilderness the way of Jehovah; make level
in the desert a highway for our God.
ISAIAH 40:3 ASV

Into the desert of my barren life enters Jehovah
and makes all the desert a garden. Into my death,
He brings His life and to my dead senses reveals
Himself the One Eternal God. Shall I not bow
before His Majesty and worship Jehovah?

THE LORD JEHOVAH

*Behold, the Lord Jehovah will come as a mighty one,
and his arm will rule for him: Behold, his reward
is with him, and his recompense before him.*

ISAIAH 40:10 ASV

The secret of all power and fullness of blessing is
in making Him the Master of our lives. Adonai
Jehovah is the Ruler, the Master. Shall we not
humbly bow at His feet and crown Him Lord of
all that we have and are?

THE EVERLASTING GOD

Hast thou not known? hast thou not heard,
that the everlasting God, the LORD, the Creator of
the ends of the earth, fainteth not, neither is weary?
There is no searching of his understanding.

ISAIAH 40:28

Everlasting, never-ending,
Age-abiding is my Lord.
Never shadow caused by turning,
Changeless, perfect, is His Word.

Everlasting God, I pray Thee,
Steady, strengthen, stablish me.
Safe from grief and pain and failure,
Hide me, Everlasting God, in Thee.

Mine Elect

Behold my servant, whom I uphold;
mine elect, in whom my soul delighteth;
I have put my spirit upon him.
ISAIAH 42:1

Infinite God, who knows and understands,
called in review all angels and all men of all the
ages and chose our Lord and called Him "Mine
Elect," to be the world's Redeemer, Savior, and
Friend. Does thy choice fall on Him? May He
be all in all to thee today.

A LIGHT OF THE GENTILES

*I the LORD have called thee in righteousness,
and will. . .give thee. . .for a light of the Gentiles.*
ISAIAH 42:6

How shall the Light lighten the Gentiles unless
we who are the light of the world shall go forth
among the Gentiles and let the light shine?
Someone brought that Light to us. Shall we not
bear it on a little farther into the darkness of
some other life?

26
MARCH

THE POLISHED SHAFT

He hath made my mouth like a sharp sword;
in the shadow of his hand hath he hid me,
and made me a polished shaft.

ISAIAH 49:2

When Christ speaks and His word cuts through our selfish lives like a sword of radiant light, let us rejoice. He who is a "Polished Shaft" speaks not only with eternal love but with unchanging faithfulness.

27
MARCH

THE HOLY ONE OF ISRAEL

Thus saith the LORD. . .Kings shall see and arise,
princes also shall worship, because of the LORD
that is faithful, and the Holy One of Israel,
and he shall choose thee.

ISAIAH 49:7

The "Holy One of Israel" could not forget His chosen people. So Israel stood and lived, and lives today because the Holy One of Israel stood beside them. And beside thy soul He stands today to be thy righteousness and lead thee to Himself.

A Root Out of
a Dry Ground

*For he shall grow up before him as a tender plant,
and as a root out of a dry ground.*
ISAIAH 53:2

Does it seem sometimes to thee that thy lot is a
hard one? He who redeemed thee knows every
difficulty, every sorrow, which thou canst feel.
Then consider Him who grew up a "Root Out
of a Dry Ground," lest ye grow weary and faint.

A MAN OF SORROWS

He is despised and rejected of men; a man of sorrows,
and acquainted with grief: and we hid
as it were our faces from him.

ISAIAH 53:3

He who was the source of all joy is also called a
"Man of Sorrows." Shall we murmur if we, too,
shall be permitted to partake of His sorrows or
to share His grief? He carries all thy sorrow and
comforts those who trust in Him.

30 MARCH

MY RIGHTEOUS SERVANT

He shall see of the travail of his soul, and shall be satisfied: by his knowledge shall my righteous servant justify many; for he shall bear their iniquities.

ISAIAH 53:11

We may bring the dropped stitches of our best weaving and the broken efforts of our best service, and laying all at His feet, rejoice that we are justified by Him who is God's "Righteous Servant."

MY MAKER

For thy Maker is thine husband.
ISAIAH 54:5

We hear of "self-made men." How rarely do we hear today the humble, joyful boast, "By the grace of God, I am what I am." All thou art that is lasting, all thou art that is good, all thou art that is helpful, God has made. Bow then before thy Maker. Worship and petition Him to finish that which He began.

THE GOD OF THE WHOLE EARTH

The LORD of hosts is his name. . .
the God of the whole earth shall he be called.
ISAIAH 54:5

Is there any part of the earth that is mine? Not till I am truly a child of the "God of the Whole Earth." May I not receive Him and possess all things in Christ and proceed to enjoy them? Not till the whole earth has heard that He is the God of the Whole Earth.

A Witness to the People

Behold, I have given him for a witness to the people.
ISAIAH 55:4

We, too, are witnesses, but oh, how full of flaws is all our testimony! He sought the Father's guidance at every step and every word. We, too, may see and hear and walk with God, and so alone shall our witness win the wanderers home.

A LEADER

*Behold, I have given him for. . .
a leader and commander to the people.*
ISAIAH 55:4

Do we realize that infinite tenderness that makes Him gently lead those who are doing the finest and the most difficult and unknown service of the world? The sorrow, the loneliness, the pain He feels with us, and gently leads us through the shadows to His own great glory.

A COMMANDER

*Behold, I have given him for a. . .
commander to the people.*
ISAIAH 55:4

Failure to obey will account for most of the
loss of communion and joy in prayer and
in the study of God's Word. If there be any
commandment which He has brought home to
our hearts which we have not obeyed, shall we
not today grant Him instant, cheerful, loving
obedience, and make Him in every detail of life
our "Commander"?

THE REDEEMER

*And the Redeemer shall come to Zion, and unto them
that turn from transgression in Jacob, saith the LORD.*
ISAIAH 59:20

When thy soul has been defeated and the race
seems hopeless, stop and think, "My Lord
redeemed me and at countless cost." If He saw
in thee that for which to pay His life, is it not
worthwhile to rise and try again, walking with
Him and worshipping Him who redeemed thee?

THINE EVERLASTING LIGHT

*Thy sun shall no more go down; neither shall thy moon
withdraw itself: for the LORD shall be thine everlasting
light, and the days of thy mourning shall be ended.*
ISAIAH 60:20

Our lives are so filled with ups and downs, with
lights and shadows, that stability seems almost
inconceivable, and everlasting darkness easier
to understand than everlasting light. Yet such is
Christ to thee. Then enter in with holy boldness
and walk in "Everlasting Light."

BALM OF GILEAD

Is there no balm in Gilead. . . ?
JEREMIAH 8:22

There are experiences of suffering through which the Master wills that we should pass. There are burdens which He does not lift, though He takes us, burden and all, into His everlasting arms. But in every suffering which He permits, He is our "Balm." He eases every pain. He comforts every sorrow. He strengthens us in every weakness.

MY PHYSICIAN

*Is there no balm in Gilead; is there no
physician there? why then is not the health
of the daughter of my people recovered?*
JEREMIAH 8:22

"Is any sick among you? Let him call for the
elders of the church and let them pray over him"
(James 5:14). He who formed us and through
whose blessing alone the human means can be
effective is our "Physician."

MY PORTION

*The portion of Jacob is not like them: for he is the former
of all things; and Israel is the rod of his inheritance:
The LORD of hosts is his name.*

JEREMIAH 10:16

Jesus is our "Portion." Shall we seek to
appropriate all of His matchless love and grace
and hope and courage and joy and fruit and
power? What more can we ask or have?

THE HOPE OF ISRAEL

*O the hope of Israel, the saviour thereof in time of trouble,
why shouldest thou be as a stranger in the land?*
JEREMIAH 14:8

The "Hope of His People," Israel, is also the
Hope of His Bride, the church. Israel shall be
regathered and become the chiefest kingdom in
all the earth. When He shall come, He shall be
both "Hope" and full fruition to every believing
soul.

RESTING PLACE

*My people hath been lost sheep: their
shepherds have caused them to go astray. . .
they have forgotten their restingplace.*

JEREMIAH 50:6

Truly there is rest for the weary, for Jesus is our
"Resting Place." In the midst of the toil and
weariness, let us hear Him who said, "Come
unto me, all ye that labour and are heavy laden,
and I will give you rest" (Matthew 11:28). To
abide in Him is to find Him our Resting Place.

THE SHEPHERD OF ISRAEL

I will set up one shepherd over them. . .
and he shall be their shepherd.
EZEKIEL 34:23

Is any name more comforting than Jesus' name of Shepherd? Feeding, leading beside still water, watching over all our wanderings, bringing us as the "Shepherd of Israel" brought His flock out of the wilderness over the Jordan into the land of peace and plenty. Teach us to trust in Thee, O Shepherd of Israel.

**13
APRIL**

FEEDER

*I will set up one shepherd over them, and he
shall feed them, even my servant David. . .
and he shall be their shepherd.*
EZEKIEL 34:23

When we have wandered from Him, He restores
our souls. What He feeds is as important for us
to learn as when and where. So let us cultivate
our appetite, our longing for His righteousness,
and we shall find He is our "Feeder."

A PLANT OF RENOWN

I will raise up for them a plant of renown, and they shall be no more consumed with hunger in the land, neither bear the shame of the heathen any more.

EZEKIEL 34:29

Although our Lord came as a tender plant, yet has He become a "Plant of Renown," for already no other name is so widely known and soon, every knee shall bow and every tongue proclaim that "Jesus Christ is Lord, to the glory of God the Father" (Philippians 2:11).

THE ANGEL OF HIS PRESENCE

*In all their affliction he was afflicted, and the angel
of his presence saved them: in his love and in his
pity he redeemed them; and he bare them,
and carried them all the days of old.*

ISAIAH 63:9

Child of God, beset by fears and troubled, let
the "Angel of His Presence" comfort thee. Speak
to Him, and thou shalt hear the voice of Him
who said, "Lo, I am with thee."

OUR POTTER

*But now, O LORD, thou art our father; we are the clay,
and thou our potter; and we all are the work of thy hand.*
ISAIAH 64:8

A beauteous, transformed life is in the Potter's
mind, and He is shaping thee through that
which seemed a rude experience. Shall we not
learn to say today, "I am the clay, and Thou the
Potter. Shape me as Thou wilt, dear Lord"?

A Righteous Branch

*Behold, the days come, saith the LORD, that I will
raise unto David a righteous Branch, and a King shall
reign and prosper, and shall execute judgment
and justice in the earth.*

Jeremiah 23:5

A "righteous branch" is one which rightly
respects, honors, and bears fruit to the tree from
which it grows. Shall we not seek with all our
hearts to so abide in Him that we shall glorify
the Father by bearing much fruit?

DAVID THEIR KING

But they shall serve the LORD their God, and David
their king, whom I will raise up unto them.
JEREMIAH 30:9

How wonderful that Christ our coming Lord
should call Himself "David Their King." What
are our thoughts and prayers concerning Israel?
Are we seeking, hoping for their King, and
telling them that He is our King, too? And
praying that their eyes may be anointed to
behold in Christ "David Their King"!

A STONE CUT OUT WITHOUT HANDS

*Thou sawest till that a stone was cut out without hands,
which smote the image upon his feet. . .and brake them
to pieces. . . . And the stone that smote the image became
a great mountain, and filled the whole earth.*

DANIEL 2:34–35

The Eternal God is planning a kingdom and
government that cannot fail, and He will smite
in His coming every man-made plan. Shall we
be ready in the day of His power?

THE ANCIENT OF DAYS

I saw in the night visions. . .one like the Son of man
came with the clouds of heaven, and came to the Ancient
of days, and they brought him near before him. . . .
His dominion is an everlasting dominion. . .
and his kingdom that which shall not be destroyed.
DANIEL 7:13–14

He was from everlasting and will be unto
the ages our Eternal God. Shall not we bow
in worship and adoration at the feet of the
"Ancient of Days"?

THE PRINCE OF PRINCES

He shall also stand up against the Prince of princes;
but he shall be broken without hand.

DANIEL 8:25

Although sitting now at the right hand of the
Father and one with Him, Christ is waiting to
be crowned on earth. Let us, in the real things
of daily life, exalt Him to His rightful place and
pour out our devotion to Him.

THE HOPE OF HIS PEOPLE

*The LORD will be the hope of his people,
and the strength of the children of Israel.*

JOEL 3:16

There is no hope in self to either be or do that
which shall bless the world; but there is glorious
hope for those who trust in Him. Jesus is the
"Hope of His People." He it is who worketh in
me "both to will and to do" (Philippians 2:13).

RULER

*But thou, Bethlehem Ephratah. . .out of thee shall
he come forth unto me that is to be ruler in Israel;
whose goings forth have been from of old.*
MICAH 5:2

Never in the history of the world has there been
such hopeless failure of human governments as
now. So must it be until He who has the right to
reign shall come and be "Ruler" in all the world.

STRONGHOLD

The LORD is good, a strong hold in the day of trouble;
and he knoweth them that trust in him.

NAHUM 1:7

There are dangerous storms which beset our
spiritual life from which there is no safe retreat
but Christ. Is He your "Stronghold"? Have you
learned to hide in Him?

WALL OF FIRE

For I, saith the LORD, will be unto her a wall of fire round about, and will be the glory in the midst of her.
ZECHARIAH 2:5

All the defense that we need is God to those who trust in Him. A "Wall of Fire" through which the fiercest foe can never come. The selfish desire that creeps through every other barricade will be consumed by Him who is a Wall of Fire when we shall hide in Him.

My Servant, the Branch

*Hear now, O Joshua the high priest, thou, and thy fellows
that sit before thee: for they are men wondered at: for,
behold, I will bring forth my servant the BRANCH.*
ZECHARIAH 3:8

Are you God's servant, serving Him as your only
Master, doing joyfully His will? If in aught you
have sought to follow any other master, will you
submit your life, your all to Him, and be His
servant now?

THE BRANCH

Thus speaketh the LORD of hosts, saying, Behold the man whose name is The BRANCH; and he shall grow up out of his place, and he shall build the temple of the LORD.

ZECHARIAH 6:12

Let us bow at His feet and remember that "apart from me, ye can do nothing" (John 15:5). Let us consider Him who, although He was the Mighty God, yet called Himself in His earthly relationship the "Branch."

KING OVER ALL THE EARTH

His feet shall stand in that day upon the mount
of Olives. . . And the LORD my God shall come,
and all the saints with thee. . . . And the LORD
shall be king over all the earth.
ZECHARIAH 14:4–5, 9

Someday all the earth shall know that He is
King. What glory, what undreamed-of wonders
shall be seen when He shall reign "over all the
earth." Does that day not allure you?

Jehovah My God

*Ye shall flee by the valley of my mountains. . .
and Jehovah my God shall come,
and all the holy ones with thee.*
ZECHARIAH 14:5 ASV

If "that thing or person who most absorbs our
thought is our God," then who is my God
today? The matchless Jehovah? Or some other
being or created thing, unworthy of my trust
and worship? Let us not rest until from our
inmost soul we cry, "Jehovah, my God."

THE KING

It shall come to pass, that every one that is
left of all the nations which came against Jerusalem
shall even go up from year to year to worship the King,
the LORD of hosts, and to keep the feast of tabernacles.

ZECHARIAH 14:16

Have we truly crowned Him in our lives? Does
He rule our words and thoughts? There will be
joy in His heart, joy in heaven, and joy in your
heart, when you shall fully crown Jesus King
and Lord of All.

THE MESSENGER OF THE COVENANT

Behold, I will send my messenger. . .even the messenger of the covenant, whom ye delight in: behold, he shall come, saith the LORD of hosts.

MALACHI 3:1

He who is our example has called Himself the "Messenger of the Covenant." The Father gave a promise to those who should believe in His Son. The Son came bringing that promise, that covenant.

REFINER

He shall sit as a refiner and purifier of silver: and he shall purify the sons of Levi. . .that they may offer unto the LORD an offering in righteousness.
MALACHI 3:3

Though through all of life we may seem to have been in the melting pot, shall we not say to Him again at any cost, "Dear Refiner, make me what Thou wilt. Refine me by any process that seemeth good unto Thee"?

PURIFIER

And he shall sit as a. . .purifier of silver.
MALACHI 3:3

No work of God shows more plainly His
boundless love than His desire to purify our
lives. The difficult experiences through which
we pass may often be understood as the infinite
love of the Father, seeking to separate the dross
from our lives, to bring us to a point of purity
where we may see and reflect His image.

THE SUN OF RIGHTEOUSNESS

But unto you that fear my name shall the Sun
of righteousness arise with healing in his wings.
MALACHI 4:2

He who walked the streets of Judea sits at the
right hand of the Father in the glory. He is the
"Sun" whose radiant righteousness heals our
sin-sick souls. Lord Jesus, we come with our
innumerable faults and infirmities and worship
Thee while we seek the "healing in Thy wings."

JESUS CHRIST

The book of the generation of Jesus Christ.
MATTHEW 1:1

Here is the first title given to our Lord in the New Testament—"Jesus Christ." One Name stands out like a radiant star to lighten all the others; one Person to whom all must render allegiance. At His feet every knee shall bow in heaven and on earth. Let us pour out our hearts to Him in praise and prayer this day, and every day.

THE SON OF DAVID

*The book of the generation of Jesus Christ,
the son of David.*
MATTHEW 1:1

Our Lord was a lineal descendant of David,
the king. This entitled Him to the right of
sovereignty over David's land, and when He was
here among men there was no other claimant
to the throne of David. Jesus Christ, "Son of
David," may our hearts be linked up with Thy
great heart always.

7 MAY

JESUS

Thou shalt call his name JESUS:
for he shall save his people from their sins.
MATTHEW 1:21

Over seven hundred times in the New
Testament is this name used—"Jesus" (Joshua).
How familiar we are with that name! He was
a type of our Lord who is our Joshua; who is
our Leader, our Protector, our Savior! Who will
never cease His lordship until He has us safely
in the sheepfold on the other side.

THE SON OF ABRAHAM

The book of the generation of Jesus Christ. . .
the son of Abraham.
MATTHEW 1:1

Abraham was the head of the covenant nation.
God had given him the promise that in his seed
should all nations be blessed. Jesus submitted to
the Jewish law in righteousness. He died for the
Jews as well as for all people. How wonderful!
God manifested in the flesh as Abraham's seed
and yet the One who made the promise to
Abraham!

EMMANUEL

*Behold, a virgin. . .shall bring forth a son,
and they shall call his name Emmanuel.*
MATTHEW 1:23

"Emmanuel," God with us! What a wonderful
Savior He is, and He is with us as He promised.
Let us sense His presence and make Him real.
Walk, talk, live with, and love Him more as
the days go by. Lord Jesus, we know that Thou
dwellest in us. May we enjoy Thy fellowship
today.

A GOVERNOR

*And thou Bethlehem. . .out of thee shall come
a Governor, that shall rule my people Israel.*
MATTHEW 2:6

Bethlehem of Judah! Who could visit this Land
of Promise and not desire to see this city of
cities, the place where Jehovah enthroned in
human form gazed into the face of the virgin
Mary, His mother. The government shall be
upon His shoulders, and He will reign in
righteousness.

THE YOUNG CHILD

When they had heard the king, they departed; and, lo, the star, which they saw in the east, went before them, till it came and stood over where the young child was.

MATTHEW 2:9

A star in the East led the wise men to a Star that outshines all the stars of heaven. Visualize, if you can, God manifested in the flesh for you. God—the "Young Child"! The Creator of all things!

A NAZARENE

And he came and dwelt in a city called Nazareth:
that it might be fulfilled which was spoken by
the prophets, He shall be called a Nazarene.
MATTHEW 2:23

On the night of His betrayal, our Lord asked
the question, "Whom seek ye?" They replied,
"Jesus of Nazareth," and He said, "I am He"
(John 18:4–5). Jesus of Nazareth, may we never
be ashamed to be called the followers of the
lowly Nazarene.

FRIEND OF SINNERS

Behold. . .a friend of publicans and sinners.
MATTHEW 11:19

Laying aside the royal robes of heaven, He came here to befriend sinful men. Let us ask ourselves the question, "Am I a friend of sinners?" If not, then I am not like my Lord, for He was and He joyed in it. Lord Jesus, the world is full of friendless sinners. May we make them acquainted with Thee who art their Friend.

THE SERVANT OF JEHOVAH

Behold my servant, whom I have chosen.
MATTHEW 12:18

Jesus, the prophesied Servant! Nothing was too great for Him to do, for He was the Creator, and nothing was too small for Him to do, for He stooped to notice a widow's mite and give a mighty lesson from it. Dear Lord, let us labor with Thee, the "Servant of Jehovah," today and thus make it a good day for Thee.

MY BELOVED

Behold. . .my beloved, in whom my soul is well pleased.
MATTHEW 12:18

God's Son was a beloved Servant. How dear
He was to the Father. Yet His love for us was
manifest in the surrender of His Son to pay the
penalty of our sin. The agony, the grief, the pain
He suffered, all had a voice which rings out the
message "God so loved."

16
MAY

A SOWER

He that soweth the good seed is the Son of man.
MATTHEW 13:37

God's Son soweth the Word of Truth in the
hearts of men. When we give out the Word
of God, we are sowing good seed. Nothing is
comparable to the Word itself. It is a living seed
and never fails. We are to imitate our Lord, the
"Sower," and see that the pure seed of the Word
is scattered wherever we go.

THE CHRIST

Thou art the Christ, the Son of the living God.
MATTHEW 16:16

This is the title of the long-looked-for Savior—
the Anointed One. From "Christ" comes the
word "Christian." Our gospel is the gospel of
Christ of which we are not ashamed, for it is the
power of God unto salvation to everyone who
believeth. Lord, let us honor Thee by having the
same anointing power resting upon us.

JESUS THE CHRIST

*Then charged he his disciples that they should
tell no man that he was Jesus the Christ.*
MATTHEW 16:20

This title, "Jesus the Christ," is used a hundred
times in the New Testament. He tells us to
go into all the world and tell all people the
wonderful message of Jesus Christ and His
finished work. Are we obeying the command?

19 MAY

MY BELOVED SON

*This is my beloved Son,
in whom I am well pleased; hear ye him.*
MATTHEW 17:5

Wonderful manifestation! A cloud of glory
overshadowing that which was too deep for
human eyes to penetrate. The voice of Jehovah
attesting that Jesus was His beloved Son
and that His words were to be heard. How
marvelous is that testimony to Him whom we
have learned to love.

**20
MAY**

THE PROPHET OF NAZARETH

This is Jesus the prophet of Nazareth of Galilee.
MATTHEW 21:11

We are all proud if we were born in some noted place; but God, when He took the form of a man, was born in a manger and made His home in Nazareth. For our sakes He became poor, that we through His poverty might be made rich. Let us meditate upon the riches of His grace. May we walk humbly this day with the despised Nazarene.

MASTER

One is your Master, even Christ;
and all ye are brethren.
MATTHEW 23:8

"Master" here means "teacher" or, some say,
"leader." The admonition is to avoid the desire
for personal distinction so common among
God's leaders. Let our eyes be fixed upon Him,
and let us depend upon the Holy Spirit who
represents Him and who guides us into all truth.
The more we seek to exalt Him, the less will we
think of magnifying ourselves.

THE BRIDEGROOM

And while they went to buy, the bridegroom came.
MATTHEW 25:10

The "Bridegroom" must come. The true church is His beloved bride. He has waited a long, long time for her to prepare herself for the glad day and to add the last one which will complete the body. Are you thinking of Him today as the Coming One?

THE HOLY ONE OF GOD

I know thee who thou art, the Holy One of God.
MARK 1:24

What a testimony coming from the lips of one possessed of an unclean spirit. But the presence of Christ overawed him. This was not a willing testimony but was forced from him. Many men are devil-possessed, and the devil has powers accorded him, but Christ can hinder his followers; can cast out his demons and forbid their speaking.

**24
MAY**

OUR BROTHER

*For whosoever shall do the will of God,
the same is my brother.*
MARK 3:35

If this is true, then the reverse is also true, and
He is our Brother. How wonderful that He
should graciously give this title to those who
do the Father's will! And what is that will? The
acceptance of His Son as our Savior and Lord,
and the submission of our will to His will as
revealed in His Word.

THOU SON OF THE MOST HIGH GOD

*And cried with a loud voice, and said,
What have I to do with thee, Jesus,
thou Son of the most high God?*
MARK 5:7

Many teachers, professors, and preachers refuse
to honor Him as the Son, but only as a Son of
God. But we lift our hearts to Him and say,
"Son of the Most High God, be our companion,
and may we withhold naught from Thee."

THE CARPENTER

Is not this the carpenter?
MARK 6:3

The "Carpenter"! We can visualize Him in His
daily tasks—a man among men. How near
He seems to us! What a joy to know that He
handled the hammer and sharpened the saw,
and helped to supply the food for the family. No
matter what our calling may be, the Carpenter
will be one with us. We can walk arm in arm
with Him to the daily task.

THE SON OF MARY

Is not this. . .the son of Mary?
MARK 6:3

We never worship Mary, but we do honor her
above all women—God's chosen vessel to bring
forth His Son and fulfill His prophecy. How
true He was to the last. Blessed title—"Son
of Mary"! The Babe who is one day to rule
the world and at whose feet we shall bow in
worshipful adoration! Let us do so now.

GOOD MASTER

*Good Master, what shall I do
that I may inherit eternal life?*
MARK 10:17

The theme of religion is do; but the theme of our Lord was just the opposite, "Follow Me." Eternal life is a gift. Those who follow Him find that He is the "Good Master" because He is the "God-Master," and He has provided for us a salvation—simple to accept but costing Him a price which involved His own life.

SON OF MAN

*The Son of man shall be delivered unto the chief
priests. . .and they shall condemn him to death.*
MARK 10:33

How difficult it is for Him to win us to Himself!
"The Son of Man" must suffer many things,
but the saddest of all was the failure of His own
disciples to enter into the burden He bore.
Oh, give us loving hearts that will enter into
fellowship with Thee in all things.

A Ransom

*The Son of man came. . .
to give his life a ransom for many.*
MARK 10:45

Here Christ is set forth as the penalty paid
for the sins of the world. As sinners under the
judgment wrath of God, He took our place
and paid the price of our deliverance with His
own blood. How precious is He to us, washed
clean in His blood and freed forever from the
punishment due us.

ONE SON, HIS WELL-BELOVED

*Having yet therefore one son, his wellbeloved,
he sent him also last unto them, saying,
They will reverence my son.*

MARK 12:6

God sent His Son, His well-beloved Son, and
they took Him and killed Him and cast Him
out. How could they? They have cast Him out
of the schools and many of the churches, though
all we have of earthly civilization and comforts
today we owe to Him.

CHRIST, THE SON OF THE BLESSED

Art thou the Christ, the Son of the Blessed?
MARK 14:61

Charges had been brought against the Lord Jesus Christ by false witnesses, but they had not agreed. The high priest put to Him a question: "Art thou the Christ, the Son of the Blessed?" And He answered, "I am." There was no denial of the title, but a straight confession of His sonship, heirship, power, and coming glory.

THE KING OF THE JEWS

Pilate asked him, Art thou the King of the Jews?
And he answering said unto them, Thou sayest it.
MARK 15:2

The Jewish people will yet proclaim Him as their own King. Let us give Him His rightful place as Ruler in our lives. How can we serve Him today? Perhaps in prayer for the Jewish people and testimony to them of the joy there is in knowing Him.

3 JUNE

THE SON OF THE HIGHEST

*He shall be great, and shall be
called the Son of the Highest.*
LUKE 1:32

Let us do our best each day to win souls for Him and thus hasten the day when we shall be with Him and reign with Him. "Son of the Highest," we bow to Thee; we worship Thee. Help us to magnify Thy name today.

GOD MY SAVIOR

My spirit hath rejoiced in God my Saviour.
LUKE 1:47

The word "Savior" here is "Soter," meaning "presence." Should we not imitate Mary in magnifying our Savior and rejoicing in the finished work which He hath wrought in our behalf? It is never what we are but what He is. Our joy is in Him. Shall we not have a tender heart for those who do not know Him?

HORN OF SALVATION

The Lord God. . .hath raised up an horn of salvation for us in the house of his servant David.
LUKE 1:68–69

The word "horn" as used in the scripture signifies "strength." In the horns, the bull manifests his strength. The Lord Jesus Christ is our Strength and a very present help in time of trouble. You may be tempted and tried today. You may have burdens to bear. Let Him be your "Horn of Salvation."

THE HIGHEST

*And thou, child, shalt be called
the prophet of the Highest.*
LUKE 1:76

Our Lord is here named the "Highest" or, better,
the "Most High." He came from the heights of
glory to be born in a manger. "Prophet" in the
New Testament means "a public expounder" and
to us has been committed this honorable title.
We are the expounders of this great revelation
of the Bible concerning our most highly exalted
Lord.

THE DAYSPRING
FROM ON HIGH

Through the tender mercy of our God;
whereby the dayspring from on high hath visited us.
LUKE 1:78

It has been suggested that the glory of the
sunrise was breaking over the hills surrounding
Jerusalem as Zacharias's lips breathed the words
inspired by the Spirit of God, "Dayspring from
On High!" Before we take up our daily tasks, let
the Holy Spirit flood our souls with the glory of
the risen Christ.

CHRIST THE LORD

*For unto you is born this day in the city of
David a Saviour, which is Christ the Lord.*
LUKE 2:11

The message was to the humble shepherds,
and it will mean much to us if we can take our
place with the shepherds, acknowledge our
unworthiness, and appropriate the truth to our
own souls—"Unto you is born a Saviour, which
is Christ the Lord." We are no longer to rule
ourselves. He is to rule us.

THE BABE

*Ye shall find the babe wrapped in swaddling clothes,
lying in a manger.*
LUKE 2:12

No other newly born babe would be found
"lying in a manger"—just One—and He, the
chiefest among ten thousand! How sad to know
that millions in our land have not yet bowed the
knee to Him. Lord, may we bow in humblest
submission to Thee today and pour out our
hearts in joyful praise to Thee, Thou Babe of
Bethlehem.

THE CONSOLATION OF ISRAEL

There was a man in Jerusalem, whose name was Simeon; and the same man was just and devout, waiting for the consolation of Israel.

LUKE 2:25

"Consolation" means "paraclete" (one coming alongside) as we think and speak of the Holy Spirit who comes to abide in and lead us out in our daily life. Lord, may we also rely upon the abiding comfort of the indwelling of the Holy Spirit all the day.

THE LORD'S CHRIST

*It was revealed unto him by the
Holy Ghost, that he should not see death,
before he had seen the Lord's Christ.*

LUKE 2:26

The Lord never fails His loved ones. When He can get hold of the hearts of men and women, He is glad to make a revelation of Himself to them and give unto them the power of the Holy Spirit. His great heart beats in sympathy with every pulsing of every loyal-hearted follower.

THE SALVATION OF GOD

For mine eyes have seen thy salvation.
LUKE 2:30

There is but one cure for the world's unrest, the "Salvation of God." Let us go out today and tell the story wherever we can. The poor, hungry-hearted, sin-sick souls are waiting. Lord, guide us in this service to Thy glory.

A Light to Lighten the Gentiles

*A light to lighten the Gentiles,
and the glory of thy people Israel.*
LUKE 2:32

What is the duty of believers? Is it not to lift the Light high so that the world of sinners in darkness may come into fellowship with Him? Lord of Light, help us to shine as lights in a dark world.

THE GLORY OF
THY PEOPLE ISRAEL

*A light to lighten the Gentiles,
and the glory of thy people Israel.*
LUKE 2:32

The Shekinah glory, manifested in the
tabernacle and temple, will shine again upon
His beloved people, and Jesus—the Jew—will
be the glory of Israel in that day. Let us love the
Jews and seek to bring the gospel of the grace of
God to them.

A Sign

This child is set. . .
for a sign which shall be spoken against.
LUKE 2:34

Our Lord Jesus Christ was a significant sign to
Israel. The prophecies had long before made
clear that Israel was to be tested when the
Messiah came. Some would believe and follow
Him. Some would reject and crucify Him. The
Sign has been given to our land, also.

THE CHILD JESUS

The child Jesus tarried behind in Jerusalem.
LUKE 2:43

Here we have our first view of Jesus as a young lad, interested in the business of His heavenly Father. Hear Him when Joseph and Mary seek Him: "Wist ye not that I must be about my Father's business?" (Luke 2:49). Let us take as a motto for our daily life the words of the Child Jesus, "I must be about my Father's business."

PHYSICIAN

And he said unto them, Ye will surely say unto
me this proverb, Physician, heal thyself.
LUKE 4:23

Our Lord is the Great Physician—"able to do
exceeding abundantly above all that we ask or
think" (Ephesians 3:20). How few know Him as
such! How few look to Him! How few depend
upon Him! Lord, Thou who art the "Great
Physician," we look to Thee today to supply our
every need.

18
JUNE

LORD OF THE SABBATH

The Son of man is Lord also of the sabbath.
LUKE 6:5

He is the Master (Lord) of the Sabbath. It is lawful to do good on the Sabbath. Solve all your problems in connection with the Sabbath Day by the question, "What would the Lord do on this day?" Then whatsoever you do, whether ye eat or drink, do all to the glory of God.

A GREAT PROPHET

*They glorified God, saying,
That a great prophet is risen up among us;
and, That God hath visited his people.*
LUKE 7:16

Jesus was a "Great Prophet." Humble, quiet, gentle, no pomp, no display, but wonderful in works. Do we recognize His greatness? Do we believe His prophecies and promises? Do we possess them and profit by them? Lord, help us to believe every word of the Prophetic Book.

THE CHRIST OF GOD

He said unto them, But whom say ye that I am?
Peter answering said, The Christ of God.
LUKE 9:20

Today the professing church is inclined to
reject the theme of Christ's atoning blood, but
those of us to whom He is the "Christ of God"
adore Him more and more as the depths of His
sacrifice and suffering are revealed.

A Certain Samaritan

But a certain Samaritan, as he journeyed. . .
had compassion on him.
LUKE 10:33

If we are indeed Spirit-born, then there must
be something of His loving-kindness in us, and
the world is waiting for our touch upon it. Will
we take the Good Samaritan for our model
today and pray, "Lord Jesus, make us more like
Thyself"?

THE MASTER OF THE HOUSE

When once the master of the house is risen up. . .
he shall answer and say unto you,
I know you not whence ye are.
LUKE 13:25

Here is a new title for our Lord—"Master of
the House." The "house" is heaven where He
is to rule. Dear Lord, may we labor and pray
earnestly today that we may be faithful in urging
upon people the necessity of decision for Christ.

A Guest

And when they saw it, they all murmured, saying,
That he was gone to be guest with a man that is a sinner.
LUKE 19:7

How we would congratulate ourselves were
some noted person to come to our house to
dine. Why do we not tell the story to everybody,
"A Great One has come to live in my house"?
"Who is He?" "He is the King of glory. He lives
with me."

A Certain Nobleman

*He said therefore, A certain nobleman went into a far
country to receive for himself a kingdom, and to return.*
LUKE 19:12

Our Lord is the "Nobleman" whose face
was turned toward the land beyond the skies
from whence He will one day return. He has
entrusted to us the most valuable treasures of
heaven—time, opportunity, the gifts of the
Holy Spirit, and a great wide world in which to
transact the greatest of all business!

THE CHOSEN OF GOD

Let him save himself,
if he be Christ, the chosen of God.
LUKE 23:35

The question mark grows as the days go by,
but the title which was given Him in derision
is a wonderfully true one. Chosen before the
foundation of the earth, and the only One
who could be chosen for the great work of our
redemption. Lord, Thou hast chosen Him, and
Thou hast chosen us.

A PROPHET MIGHTY IN DEED AND WORD

And he said unto them, What things? And they said unto him, Concerning Jesus of Nazareth, which was a prophet mighty in deed and word before God and all the people.

LUKE 24:19

Mighty in life, mighty in death, and mighty in His resurrection! He lives in the hearts of millions. He will live throughout the eternal ages, and every word He ever uttered will be fulfilled to the letter.

27 JUNE

THE WORD

In the beginning was the Word,
and the Word was with God, and the Word was God.
JOHN 1:1

What a foundation for our faith when we know that Jesus was the Word and the Word was God. Without Him—nothing! With Him—all things! Oh Thou Living Word, who hast given us the written Word, help us to abide in Thee today.

THE LIGHT OF MEN

In him was life; and the life was the light of men.
JOHN 1:4

We have the Light of life. We see Him face-
to-face. We bask in the sunshine of His glory.
Pity the blind! Pray for the blind! Carry the
light of the glorious gospel to their darkened
souls. Tell them to arise and shine, for the
Light is come and the glory of the Lord shall
shine upon them.

THE TRUE LIGHT

That was the true Light, which
lighteth every man that cometh into the world.
JOHN 1:9

The gloom of sin, the uncertainty of life, the dark outlook for the future, confront the sinner stumbling along without God and without hope. God has ordained us as lights. Let our lights shine today, and may we help some blinded ones to see Jesus as the "True Light" of the world.

THE ONLY BEGOTTEN
OF THE FATHER

*And the Word was made flesh, and dwelt among us,
(and we beheld his glory, the glory as of the only
begotten of the Father,) full of grace and truth.*

JOHN 1:14

Christ is the Unique Figure in the world's
history—the sinless, perfect One—perfect God
and perfect Man. He must be God to forgive
sin, and He must be Man to atone for sin. So
the God-Man is our Savior.

THE LAMB OF GOD

*The next day John seeth Jesus coming unto him,
and saith, Behold the Lamb of God,
which taketh away the sin of the world.*
JOHN 1:29

No one else could be God's Lamb. He was the voluntary offering. What can we do? Believe it, accept it, take our place with Him. Let us behold Thee every day, counting nothing too good to give to Thee or too much to do for Thee.

THE SON OF GOD

And I saw, and bare record that this is the Son of God.
JOHN 1:34

Jesus is God's Son. He is the Promised One.
We should seek to be like John the Baptist—a
signpost pointing to Him and saying, "Behold!
the Son of God." May we be willing to suffer
anything so that our testimony shall be clear and
clean always for Him.

RABBI

Nathanael answered and saith unto him,
Rabbi, thou art the Son of God.
JOHN 1:49

"Rabbi" means "teacher." Nathanael recognized Christ as a teacher, and He was—the greatest Teacher who ever lived. He taught the truth. He condescended to men of low estate. He used words which men could understand. He illustrated His messages in a practical manner.

THE KING OF ISRAEL

*Nathanael answered and saith unto him, Rabbi. . .
thou art the King of Israel.*
JOHN 1:49

When Nathanael came in touch with Jesus,
he broke out in testimony to His deity and
His messiahship. Our Lord did not fail to
acknowledge this sterling testimony. Ministering
spirits were to be seen by him. We also can see
the open heavens if we have faith.

HIS ONLY BEGOTTEN SON

For God so loved the world, that he gave his only begotten Son, that whosoever believeth in him should not perish, but have everlasting life.
JOHN 3:16

Here is the most beloved verse in the Bible. Oh, the wonders of such a love! How we should love our Lord Jesus Christ—God's "Only Begotten Son"! Let us with throbbing hearts for a lost world go forth to tell the story to sinful, suffering men.

THE GIFT OF GOD

*Jesus answered. . .If thou knewest the gift of God,
and who it is that saith to thee, Give me to drink;
thou wouldest have asked of him, and he
would have given thee living water.*

JOHN 4:10

Christ is God's gift to us. What is our gift to
Him? May we yield ourselves to Him! May we
imitate the Samaritan woman and go forth with
the message: Come, see a Man—God's Gift.

7
JULY

MESSIAH

The woman saith unto him,
I know that Messias cometh, which is called Christ:
when he is come, he will tell us all things.
JOHN 4:25

This woman was the last one we would have chosen for such a revelation—but her soul was filled at once with the Spirit of life and hope, and her lips bore a testimony bringing salvation to a multitude. Oh, that our lips might bear such convincing, convicting, and converting testimony.

THE CHRIST, THE SAVIOR OF THE WORLD

*We have heard him ourselves,
and know that this is indeed the Christ,
the Saviour of the world.*

JOHN 4:42

"We have heard him ourselves." The need of the world today is the personal experience of believers manifested in a personal devotion to Christ and in personal testimony to a hungry-hearted world. O "Christ, Savior of the World," baptize us with the spirit of service for Thee!

9
JULY

THE TRUE BREAD
FROM HEAVEN

My Father giveth you the true bread from heaven.
JOHN 6:32

Jesus is the "True Bread from Heaven" of which,
if men partake, they live forever. He only can
satisfy our soul's hunger. The world is starving
for the True Bread. Lord Jesus, help us to go
forth today and feed some hungry souls.

10 JULY

THE BREAD OF GOD

*For the bread of God is he which cometh down
from heaven, and giveth life unto the world.*
JOHN 6:33

The Bread of God is a gift to hungry humanity.
Teachers, preachers, and workers for the Lord
must always bear this in mind: The unsaved are
hungry. Nothing will ever satisfy their hunger
but the "Bread of God"—Jesus Christ.

THE BREAD OF LIFE

Jesus said unto them, I am the bread of life:
he that cometh to me shall never hunger;
and he that believeth on me shall never thirst.

JOHN 6:35

Jesus is the Bread of Life. It must be made known to an ignorant world. There is nothing to do but to believe—receive—accept. Nothing more. Lord, help us to go out laden with the "Bread of Life" and give it to the hungry.

12
JULY

THE LIVING BREAD

*I am the living bread which
came down from heaven.*
JOHN 6:51

Our Lord tells us that He will lay down His
own life in order that we may have this "Living
Bread" to eat and so live forever. The process
by which we are to nourish the new nature
which we received by accepting Him is by
feeding on Him.

13
JULY

THE LIGHT OF THE WORLD

Then spake Jesus again unto them, saying,
I am the light of the world: he that followeth me shall
not walk in darkness, but shall have the light of life.
JOHN 8:12

The world is a dark, gloomy place, but if we
follow Him we shall not walk in darkness.
Walking in the light, we have fellowship with
one another and reflect the glory of His person
in the gloom of the world.

I Am

*Jesus said unto them, Verily, verily,
I say unto you, Before Abraham was, I am.*
JOHN 8:58

There is no time limit to the life of our Lord.
He is the Eternal Son of God. Before the
creation of the world, He was the "I Am!" After
the world passes away, He will still be the "I
Am." Without Him, nothing was made that was
made. He is God!

THE DOOR OF THE SHEEP

Then said Jesus unto them again, Verily, verily,
I say unto you, I am the door of the sheep.
JOHN 10:7

Our Lord is the door by which entrance is gained to heaven. Put your hand upon the door—Jesus Christ on the cross—and enter the fold. There is food for the sheep, and water and rest. Free from Satan's snare, filled with joy and peace, what more could we ask or desire?

THE GOOD SHEPHERD

*I am the good shepherd: the good shepherd
giveth his life for the sheep.*

JOHN 10:11

If we could stop for a few moments and sense
His presence, longing to speak to us in tones of
deepest love, would we not say of Him, "He is
so good. He died for me"? And would not our
hearts go out in passionate love to Him? Loving
Shepherd, help us to keep close to Thee today.

17
JULY

ONE SHEPHERD

Other sheep I have, which are not of this fold:
them also I must bring, and they shall hear my voice;
and there shall be one fold, and one shepherd.
JOHN 10:16

Our Lord had a heart boundless in love; a soul
longing for the children of men; looking into
the future, seeing the cross, and the many sheep,
washed in the same blood, filled with the same
Holy Spirit of life, folded in the one fold.

THE RESURRECTION

*Jesus said unto her, I am the resurrection,
and the life: he that believeth in me,
though he were dead, yet shall he live.*

JOHN 11:25

Faith in our Lord equals eternal life, and that
assures our resurrection. Because He lives,
we must live. He who raised up Christ from
the dead shall quicken our bodies. In His
resurrection He conquered death.

THE CHRIST, THE SON OF GOD

She saith unto him, Yea, Lord:
I believe that thou art the Christ, the Son of God.
JOHN 11:27

Here is a remarkable confession from the lips of Martha. Lazarus was in the tomb. Her eyes, no doubt, were full of tears, but her faith in Jesus as the Christ never wavered. Lord Jesus, help us never to disappoint Thee in our faith in Thy power and Thy promise to answer our faith.

A GRAIN OF WHEAT

*Jesus answered them, saying, The hour is come,
that the Son of man should be glorified. Verily, verily,
I say unto you, Except a corn [grain] of wheat fall into
the ground and die, it abideth alone: but if it die,
it bringeth forth much fruit.*

JOHN 12:23–24

He must die in order to bring forth fruit. So
must we, if we are to be like Him. Look upon
His example. Do we desire to be like Him?

MASTER

Ye call me Master and Lord:
and ye say well; for so I am.
JOHN 13:13

"Master" means "teacher," and the authoritative Teacher He was and is. He has left to us His words of wisdom, and we are to sit at His feet and learn of Him. We recognize this position of our Lord by yielding submission to His authority and acknowledging it daily.

THE WAY

Jesus saith unto him, I am the way.
JOHN 14:6

He is the only "Way" which leads directly to the
Father. There are a thousand ways which lead to
destruction, to eternal darkness and separation
from the Father. When we walk in the Way,
we walk in the light. We journey with Him in
sweet fellowship. The Way is lightened by His
countenance. He holds us by the hand. He
supplies our needs.

THE TRUTH

Jesus saith unto him, I am. . .the truth.
JOHN 14:6

We are God's free men, for we know Him who is the "Truth," and the Truth makes us free. He is the Truth about the Word of God. Doubt concerning the inerrancy of the Bible is a doubt concerning Himself. Lord, Thou art the Truth. We look to Thee. Guide us into the Truth all the days.

The Life

Jesus saith unto him, I am. . .the life.
JOHN 14:6

He is the "Life"—Eternal Life, the Author of
Life, and the Giver of Life. We almost stagger
when we confront this statement by the One
who left heaven and came to this earth that He
might reveal Himself and receive to Himself
those who were to inherit through Him and
share with Him this Eternal Life.

25
JULY

THE VINE

I am the vine, ye are the branches:
He that abideth in me, and I in him, the same bringeth
forth much fruit: for without me ye can do nothing.
JOHN 15:5

Here the Lord calls Himself the "Vine" as He
associates Himself with the branches. He is the
root and stem upon which we, as branches,
must depend. We can bear no fruit of ourselves.
Our dependence is upon Him.

THE OVERCOMER

I have overcome the world.
JOHN 16:33

How blessed to be in Him who is the Source
of our strength! We must learn to overcome
through Him. There is nothing too hard for
Him. He loves to give us victory. We please Him
by trusting Him and taking by faith what He has
purchased for us. Let us commit all to Him for
victory today and thus glorify our Overcomer.

OUR KEEPER

*While I was with them in the world, I kept them
in thy name: those that thou gavest me I have kept.*
JOHN 17:12

Satan would separate us, if he could, from our
Lord; but the Lord is our Keeper and we can
trust in His unfailing promise: "[I] will him
keep in perfect peace whose mind is stayed on
[me] because he trusteth in [me]" (Isaiah 26:3).
Nothing can separate us from the love of God.

THE SENT OF THE FATHER

*As thou hast sent me into the world,
even so have I also sent them into the world.*
JOHN 17:18

He was God's "Sent One." He was set apart
for the work of redemption. He prays that His
disciples might also be set apart for the great
work of saving men. His holy desire is that we
might be in the world with the same message
that He Himself had.

THE MAN

Behold the man!
JOHN 19:5

"Behold the Man!" For our sakes—in order to be one with us and to bear our sin—He threw aside His royal vesture and donned the garments of humanity, that He might interpret to us the purpose of the Father. In the name of this Man, our Father, we ask for guidance today and pray that our hearts may be in tune with His.

30
JULY

My Lord and My God

Thomas answered and said unto him,
My LORD and my God.
JOHN 20:28

How sympathetically loving is our Lord
with our unbelief, yet how He longs for our
unquestioning faith. Let us honor Him by
believing Him with all our heart. Our Lord
and our God, help us today to look upon the
wounds which Thou carriest for us and with full
faith renew our pledge of loyalty to Thee.

31
JULY

A Man Approved of God

Jesus of Nazareth, a man approved of God
among you by miracles and wonders and signs.
Acts 2:22

He professed to be the promised Messiah
and made good His profession by His public
life. His miraculous works were the proof of
miraculous power. When believers are anointed
of the Holy Spirit and seek to honor their Lord,
the approval of God the Father will be upon
them.

THINE HOLY ONE

Because thou wilt not leave my soul in hell, neither wilt thou suffer thine Holy One to see corruption.
ACTS 2:27

It was impossible that Christ should be holden by the power of death. He passed through the agony, but death could not hold Him. He hath broken the bars of death from us, and in the freedom of the new life, with glorified bodies, we will be forever with Him.

THE HOLY ONE
AND THE JUST

But ye denied the Holy One and the Just,
and desired a murderer to be granted unto you.
ACTS 3:14

Do we recognize him as the Holy One? Every suggestion of the "Holy One" should stir our souls in adoration and holy desire to be like Him. O Thou Holy One, may we seek earnestly this day to live as in Thy sight, adoring Thee constantly.

THE PRINCE OF LIFE

And [ye] killed the Prince of life, whom God hath raised from the dead; whereof we are witnesses.
ACTS 3:15

He came that men might have life and life more abundantly. Are we doing our best to make Him known to lost men? Lord Jesus, Thou "Prince of Life," stir our hearts with compassion for the lost and help us today to make Thee known to some blinded soul.

THE HOLY CHILD JESUS

For of a truth against thy holy child Jesus, whom thou hast anointed, both Herod, and Pontius Pilate, with the Gentiles, and the people of Israel, were gathered together.
ACTS 4:27

Peter and John reported what had been done and the assembly glorified the name of the "Holy Child Jesus" against whom His enemies were gathered. They prayed that in the name of this Holy Child Jesus, signs and wonders might be wrought, and they were.

A Prince and a Savior

*Him hath God exalted with his right
hand to be a Prince and a Saviour.*
ACTS 5:31

To establish His title, He became the Sin-
Bearer that He might become the Sin-Blotter.
Destined to deepest depths of human suffering
and humility, but raised to the highest heights
of honor and glory. Lord Jesus, our "Prince and
our Savior," we yield ourselves to Thee with glad
hearts.

THE JUST ONE

*Which of the prophets have not your fathers persecuted?
and they have slain them which shewed before
of the coming of the Just One; of whom ye have
been now the betrayers and murderers.*

ACTS 7:52

The words "Just (or Righteous) One" burst
from the lips of Stephen, the first martyr. He
paid with his life for his loyalty to his Lord and
will receive his reward. How much would we be
willing to suffer for Him?

LORD JESUS

*And they stoned Stephen, calling upon God,
and saying, Lord Jesus, receive my spirit.*
ACTS 7:59

Stephen is passing through the fire of Jewish
hatred. But God is faithful to His faithful
servant and martyr and opens the heavens to
him, showing him Jesus standing at the right of
His glory. The cry of Stephen was "Lord Jesus,
receive my spirit." What a testimony to the
deity of our Lord!

AUGUST

LORD OF ALL

The word which God sent unto the children of Israel,
preaching peace by Jesus Christ: (he is Lord of all).
ACTS 10:36

Jesus Christ is Lord of all men. He commissions
us to go and preach to all. The world is the field,
and every soul living has a claim upon us. O
"Lord of All," fill us with the Holy Ghost that
we may gladly be witnesses to all men.

THE JUDGE OF QUICK AND DEAD

*He commanded us to preach unto the people,
and to testify that it is he which was ordained of
God to be the Judge of quick and dead.*
ACTS 10:42

It must not be forgotten that Christ is the
Judge of all men. Believers have rights conferred
upon them by reason of their acceptance of the
sacrifice of Jesus Christ, but they, too, must face
Him to be judged for their works.

THAT MAN WHOM HE HATH ORDAINED

*Because he hath appointed a day,
in the which he will judge the world in righteousness
by that man whom he hath ordained.*

ACTS 17:31

Jesus was ordained as the Man who is to judge the whole human race. It will be a righteous judgment by a righteous Judge. He will have the books opened before Him. What is your relation to this Ordained Man? Are you ready?

JESUS OF NAZARETH

*And I answered, Who art thou, Lord?
And he said unto me, I am Jesus of
Nazareth, whom thou persecutest.*
ACTS 22:8

More than twenty times in the scriptures is our
Lord called "Jesus of Nazareth." That is His
name now. From the glory He acknowledges His
earthly title—"Jesus of Nazareth." Jesus is God.
He made the worlds, but He acknowledges the
little obscure town of Nazareth, His hometown
down here.

JESUS CHRIST OUR LORD

*As sin hath reigned unto death,
even so might grace reign through righteousness
unto eternal life by Jesus Christ our Lord.*
ROMANS 5:21

Sin wore the crown of victory over man, but
there was One greater than Satan, and in that
One was manifested the victorious power of
grace (unmerited favor) by which, through the
sacrifice of Jesus Christ, God's condescending
love could be manifested in His Son, our Lord
and Master.

The Firstborn among Many Brethren

For whom he did foreknow, he also did predestinate to be conformed to the image of his Son, that he might be the firstborn among many brethren.
ROMANS 8:29

Jesus is the "Firstborn," and we who are "born-again" ones are, by His grace, being conformed to His image, and when He comes from heaven, we will be among the sons of God and united forever to and with Him.

HIS OWN SON

*He that spared not his own Son,
but delivered him up for us all, how shall he
not with him also freely give us all things?*
ROMANS 8:32

Having given us His best, will He withhold
anything from us? Why do we live such poor,
selfish, sordid lives, when the world is so needy,
when hearts are so heavy and broken? Why do
we fail to appropriate what He has so freely
offered us?

GOD BLESSED FOREVER

*Whose are the fathers, and of whom as concerning
the flesh Christ came, who is over all,
God blessed for ever. Amen.*
ROMANS 9:5

As we journey through the Word of God, how
Christ illumines it with His presence! How
significant is this title "God Blessed Forever"!
May we bow to Him today and say from our
hearts, "To us Thou art indeed 'God Blessed
Forever.'"

LORD OVER ALL

*For there is no difference between the Jew
and the Greek: for the same Lord over all
is rich unto all that call upon him.*

ROMANS 10:12

"He is rich unto all who call upon him." The
only requirement is that we belong to His
family, and for the family there are riches of
revelation, forgiveness, grace, and love. Just call
in His name, and He will answer. He will supply
all your need.

THE LORD

*For whosoever shall call upon the name
of the Lord shall be saved.*

ROMANS 10:13

How many sin-sick, weary souls there are who
are hungry for salvation. They would gladly cry
to the Lord, but He has not been revealed to
them. They need someone to tell them of His
longing to have them in His family. O Lord,
our Master, send us all out today to tell the love
story to others.

THE DELIVERER

*So all Israel shall be saved: as it is written,
There shall come out of Sion the Deliverer,
and shall turn away ungodliness from Jacob.*
ROMANS 11:26

Let us never forget how much we owe to the
Jewish race, and let us seek earnestly to bring as
many of them as possible to Christ now. O Lord
Jesus, Thou hast been our "Deliverer." Help us
to help others to know Thee.

LORD BOTH OF THE DEAD AND LIVING

For to this end Christ both died, and rose, and revived,
that he might be Lord both of the dead and living.
ROMANS 14:9

Christ is the center of all affairs as related to this earth. One day saints and sinners will be judged for their manner of living. There can be no evasions, no exceptions. All accounts must be faced and settled. Men should live in that prospect.

MINISTER OF
THE CIRCUMCISION

*Now I say that Jesus Christ was a
minister of the circumcision for the truth of God,
to confirm the promises made unto the fathers.*

ROMANS 15:8

He came to the Jews with His message of love,
but they would not have Him. He turned to the
Gentiles and some received Him. The gospel
of Jesus Christ is for all men, because all have
sinned. He longs to gather all unto Himself.

THE POWER OF GOD

*But unto them which are called,
both Jews and Greeks, Christ the power of God.*
1 CORINTHIANS 1:24

When we think of our Lord Jesus Christ, we can visualize Him as the Mighty One. He is the "Power of God," for all power is committed unto Him. He speaks and it is done! And this Powerful One has said, "Ask, and ye shall receive" (John 16:24). How wonderful that He should love such as we!

THE WISDOM OF GOD

*But unto them which are called, both Jews
and Greeks, Christ. . .the wisdom of God.*
1 CORINTHIANS 1:24

To those who are called, He is the "Wisdom
of God." The Bible teaches us that wisdom is
the principal thing and, therefore, we should
seek wisdom and Him who is the storehouse of
wisdom. Let us be wise and seek the wisdom
that passeth all understanding.

RIGHTEOUSNESS

*But of him are ye in Christ Jesus,
who of God is made unto us. . .righteousness.*
1 CORINTHIANS 1:30

There was nothing in us that would commend
us to God and never could be. But what a
change when we are in Him and He is in us. We
are made sinless in Him, for He bore all our sins
and paid all the penalty, and His righteousness is
imputed to us.

24
AUGUST

SANCTIFICATION

But of him are ye in Christ Jesus,
who of God is made unto us. . .sanctification.
1 CORINTHIANS 1:30

To be "sanctified" is to be set apart. We are in
Christ Jesus, and what He is, we are; and what
He has, we share. O Lord, we are nothing. Thou
art everything. Thou hast set us apart to be Thy
representatives in a lost world. In every act and
deed we represent Thee.

REDEMPTION

But of him are ye in Christ Jesus,
who of God is made unto us. . .redemption.
1 CORINTHIANS 1:30

The grace of God is wonderful. He gave His
Son for our redemption, and that Son poured
out His lifeblood to atone for our sins. Who
could measure the height or depth or length or
breadth of such love? Shall we not manifest our
love by yielding all that we are and have to Him?

THE LORD OF GLORY

Which none of the princes of this world knew:
for had they known it, they would not
have crucified the Lord of glory.
1 CORINTHIANS 2:8

Oh, the pity of it that hearts are bolted against the revelation of our Lord who descended from the heights of glory. Pity the poor princes of this world who resist the entreaties of the Holy Spirit to receive Him.

THE FOUNDATION

*For other foundation can no man lay
than that is laid, which is Jesus Christ.*
1 CORINTHIANS 3:11

"Jesus Christ, the Foundation." Upon this
Foundation is built all of the purposes of God
for time and for eternity. Upon it is being built
the church. How is this structure to be built? By
the Holy Spirit through His disciples who are
endowed with power to go into the world and
gather the stones of human souls.

28
AUGUST

OUR PASSOVER

Purge out therefore the old leaven,
that ye may be a new lump, as ye are unleavened.
For even Christ our passover is sacrificed for us.
1 CORINTHIANS 5:7

The Jews had their Passover which commemorated their flight from Egypt. It was a foretaste of our "Passover"—a Lamb without blemish, slain for our sins, whose blood sprinkled upon our hearts cleanses from sin, and whose broken body feeds our souls.

THAT SPIRITUAL ROCK

And did all drink the same spiritual drink:
for they drank of that spiritual Rock that followed them:
and that Rock was Christ.

1 CORINTHIANS 10:4

The children of Israel were supernaturally
supplied daily with food and water. The water
was a gift from God, symbolizing the Water
of Life which springs from the spiritual Rock,
which is Christ. Lord Jesus, our spiritual Rock,
help us to drink freely of Thy living water today.

30
AUGUST

THE HEAD OF EVERY MAN

But I would have you know,
that the head of every man is Christ.
1 CORINTHIANS 11:3

God reigns supreme in this world, but God is
manifested in the flesh in the person of Jesus,
who is supreme over all humanity. As Head of
the church He has given orders to "go ye into all
the world and preach the gospel" (Mark 16:15).
Let every one of us seek to do our part.

THE FIRSTFRUITS OF
THEM THAT SLEEP

*But now is Christ risen from the dead,
and become the firstfruits of them that slept.*
1 CORINTHIANS 15:20

The Bible, the lives of believers, all witness to
the fact of His resurrection. He is the firstfruits,
and every believer looks forward with glad
anticipation to the coming day of all days when
the trumpet shall sound and "the dead in Christ
shall rise first."

THE LAST ADAM

*And so it is written, The first man Adam
was made a living soul; the last Adam
was made a quickening spirit.*

1 CORINTHIANS 15:45

The first Adam was created out of the dust of
the earth. The last Adam was conceived by the
Holy Ghost. He was a "God-Man." He was a
life-giving Spirit. Through this last Adam, we
receive the nature which qualifies us for the
celestial joys of the celestial city.

A QUICKENING SPIRIT

*And so it is written. . .
the last Adam was made a quickening spirit.*
1 CORINTHIANS 15:45

How wonderful is the operation of God in creating in fallen man an eternal life! These mortal bodies shall become glorious, immortal bodies in which He will dwell throughout the eternal years. What a glorious outlook for us whose eyes are turned heavenward from whence we look for Him.

THE LORD FROM HEAVEN

*The first man is of the earth, earthy;
the second man is the Lord from heaven.*

1 CORINTHIANS 15:47

The contrast here again is between Adam and
Christ. The first man was a failure, and all men
are born in sin and are failures. Therefore, the
necessity of a "Man from heaven." All men bear
the image of the earthly, but to bear the image
of the heavenly, Christ should be their desire.

4
SEPTEMBER

THE IMAGE OF GOD

The god of this world hath blinded the minds of them which believe not, lest the light of the glorious gospel of Christ, who is the image of God, should shine unto them.

2 CORINTHIANS 4:4

As the coming of the Lord draws near, Satan's blinding powers are more manifest. This fact should stir our hearts to intensified purpose to present to the unsaved, Jesus, the "Image of God."

5

SEPTEMBER

THE UNSPEAKABLE GIFT

Thanks be to God for his unspeakable gift.
2 CORINTHIANS 9:15 ASV

There was no treasure which God could give comparable to the gift of His Son. How could it be possible that the Father would give to sinners the Son of His love? How we ought to love Him! Is there anything we have or are that we would withhold from Him?

CHRIST

Blessed be the God and Father of our Lord Jesus Christ, who hath blessed us with all spiritual blessings in heavenly places in Christ.
EPHESIANS 1:3

God showers His blessings upon His people. What are the spiritual blessings in Christ? They are spiritual gifts, the blessing of the gospel—the "good news" from God. They include the eternal purpose and precious promises of God which are to be manifested now, in the future, and throughout eternity.

HEAD OVER ALL THINGS

And hath put all things under his feet,
and gave him to be the head over all things to the church.
EPHESIANS 1:22

The gift of God to the church was Christ. We
need to recognize our exalted position, chosen
in Him before the world was, dear as the apple
of His eye. Let us live in the assurance that
through the endless ages we shall be His blessed,
beloved ones.

HE THAT FILLETH ALL IN ALL

[The church,] which is his body,
the fulness of him that filleth all in all.
EPHESIANS 1:23

The church is the "fullness of Christ." Christ could never be complete without the church, and the church could never be complete until the last member is brought into the body. Therefore, the business of the church is to be busy seeking to save the lost.

OUR PEACE

*For he is our peace, who hath made both one,
and hath broken down the middle
wall of partition between us.*
EPHESIANS 2:14

Thank God, we have everything in Him. In the poor, old world, we have tribulations, trials, disappointments, sorrows of all kinds, but there never will be a time when we may not pillow our heads upon His shoulder and be at peace.

10
SEPTEMBER

ONE LORD

One Lord, one faith, one baptism. . .
EPHESIANS 4:5

The apostle is stating in this and the succeeding verses a great truth concerning the church. There is a sevenfold unity. We are not our own. We were bought with a great price. We are His subjects, under His rule and authority. Lord Jesus, let us bow to Thee as the one Lord, and with loyal hearts yield to Thy authority.

THE HEAD

But speaking the truth in love, may [we] grow up into him in all things, which is the head, even Christ.
EPHESIANS 4:15

We have already viewed Christ as the "Head over All Things," but here we have Him as the Head of the church. There is inspiration in this thought—that we are to grow up into Him. How are we to do this? The Head dominates the body, and according to the need, the supply is furnished.

AN OFFERING

*And walk in love, as Christ also hath loved us,
and hath given himself for us an offering.*
EPHESIANS 5:2

He became sin for us. No man could take His
life without His consent, who through the
Eternal Spirit offered Himself without spot to
God. Lord Jesus, we recognize Thy offering in
our behalf. Help us to walk in love as Thou hast
also loved us.

A Sacrifice to God

And walk in love, as Christ also hath loved us,
and hath given himself. . .a sacrifice to God.
EPHESIANS 5:2

God's holiness and righteousness demanded
some way by which sin could be forgiven
and removed, so that sinful men could live in
fellowship with Him. There was only one way.
Through His sacrifice, our sins were washed
away and rights and titles to heaven granted us.

A Sweet-Smelling Savor

*And walk in love, as Christ also hath loved us,
and hath given himself. . .for a sweetsmelling savour.*
EPHESIANS 5:2

When Christ laid down His life on the cross,
what a perfume went up to God—the perfume
from the sacrifice of His Son! Has the perfume
of the cross yet reached you? It reached heaven.
Has the love of God, as manifested in the
sacrifice of His Son, mastered you?

A SERVANT

*But [Christ Jesus] made himself of no reputation,
and took upon him the form of a servant,
and was made in the likeness of men.*
PHILIPPIANS 2:7

He was God manifest in the flesh, but He made
Himself of "no reputation." As a servant, Christ
humbled Himself. From what lofty heights—
Creator of all things down to a servant of men.
What an example for us is He—the Servant!

16

SEPTEMBER

THE LORD JESUS CHRIST

To the saints and faithful brethren in Christ which are at Colosse: Grace be unto you, and peace, from God our Father and the Lord Jesus Christ.

COLOSSIANS 1:2

Hundreds of names and titles are given to Him, but after all, He has said, "I and my Father are one" (John 10:30). When He descends from heaven we will see Him in whom all of these titles are vested.

HIS DEAR SON

*[The Father] hath delivered us from the
power of darkness, and hath translated
us into the kingdom of his dear Son.*
COLOSSIANS 1:13

Millions are doomed to eternal darkness. There
is but One who can deliver men. It is "His Dear
Son." We are the possessors of this truth. How
can we be indifferent to the blinded souls all
around us when His dear Son is longing to have
them respond to His call, "Come unto Me"?

THE IMAGE OF
THE INVISIBLE GOD

[The Son] is the image of the invisible God.
COLOSSIANS 1:15

It is difficult for us to refrain from loud acclamation as we view this expression concerning our Lord, the very "Image of the Invisible God"! We look at Him and we see God. We hear His voice and we hear God. Glory to God in the highest! We know Him. We love Him. We wait with longing hearts for Him.

THE FIRSTBORN OF EVERY CREATURE

[The Son is] the firstborn of every creature.
COLOSSIANS 1:15

So many statements in scripture make plain the fact that God and Christ are One. He is the manifestation of God. The invisible God has become visible to men in Jesus Christ; He is the Head of the natural creation and of the new creation, so that He is intimately allied to us.

CREATOR OF ALL THINGS

For by him were all things created.
COLOSSIANS 1:16

He is the Creator of all things—visible and invisible! Are we not prone to underestimate Him and undervalue His work? Should we not take a place lower than Paul who counted himself the least of all saints? Lord, help us. Keep ambition and pride from dominating us. Keep us at Thy feet in worship and praise. Amen.

THE HEAD OF THE BODY

He is the head of the body, the church.
COLOSSIANS 1:18

The church is His Body. We are members
of that Body. We are one with Him. What
is involved in this? We must recognize our
relationship and think of Him always as
our Head and look to Him for wisdom and
guidance.

THE BEGINNING

[He] is the beginning, the firstborn from the dead.
COLOSSIANS 1:18

He is the "Beginning." Who is? The "Firstborn from the Dead." By His resurrection, He inaugurated a new era, the beginning of a new life—eternal life. He is the Prince of life. He solved the problem of sin forever. He rose from the dead. He conquered death. His resurrection assures the resurrection of the bodies of all those who sleep in Him.

THE FIRSTBORN FROM THE DEAD

He is. . .the firstborn from the dead;
that in all things he might have the preeminence.
COLOSSIANS 1:18

He is the Originator of spiritual life. Through death, He paid the penalty for sin and was raised for our justification "from among the dead." Lord Jesus, we glorify Thy name as the "Firstborn from the Dead" and look forward to the day when we also shall be raised and abide with Thee forever.

HOPE OF GLORY

*To whom God would make known what is the riches
of the glory of this mystery among the Gentiles;
which is Christ in you, the hope of glory.*
COLOSSIANS 1:27

This glory which is so wonderful is the garment
with which all believers will be clothed when
Christ comes for us. How we should prize the
possession of "Christ in us." Do we, and do we
long that others might possess it also?

CHRIST OUR LIFE

When Christ, who is our life, shall appear,
then shall ye also appear with him in glory.
COLOSSIANS 3:4

When he shall appear, He shall change these bodies and fashion them like unto His own glorious body. He is preparing a place for us. He is coming for us. The anticipation of this is the great incentive of our life. No condition in life here can rob us of the joy of this great truth.

ALL AND IN ALL

*Where there is neither Greek nor Jew,
circumcision nor uncircumcision, Barbarian,
Scythian, bond nor free: but Christ is all, and in all.*
COLOSSIANS 3:11

Christ is the Creator of all things. He is in all
things. He is the beginning and the end of all
things. He is the criterion by which all things
must be measured. All power is in Him. All
dominion, all authority is vested in Him.

THE LORD CHRIST

Knowing that of the Lord ye shall receive the reward of the inheritance: for ye serve the Lord Christ.
COLOSSIANS 3:24

We are servants of the "Lord Christ." Earthly masters will disappoint us; our heavenly Master—never! No greater privilege was ever accorded to men than that of serving the Lord Christ. We are heirs to a wonderful inheritance, and our portion will be assigned to us.

28

SEPTEMBER

LORD OF PEACE

*Now the Lord of peace himself give you peace
always by all means. The Lord be with you all.*

2 THESSALONIANS 3:16

Our Lord is the Author of peace. In order to
have this wonderful peace we must be yoked up
close to Him. We live in a world of unrest and
conflict. "No peace for the wicked!" They can
never know Him unless He is revealed to them.
Let us cheerfully make Him manifest today.

29
SEPTEMBER

OUR HOPE

Paul, an apostle of Jesus Christ
by the commandment of God our Saviour,
and Lord Jesus Christ, which is our hope.

1 TIMOTHY 1:1

He is our "Hope." His promises assure us and fix our faith upon Him. He is the center of the life of a true believer. What could be more satisfying after a day of toil and burden-bearing than to remember how His Word was our comfort and His promises our peace?

CHRIST JESUS

*Christ Jesus came into the world to
save sinners; of whom I am chief.*
1 TIMOTHY 1:15

Mankind is under the curse of sin and has no
power to atone for its sin. God alone could meet
the issue and solve the problem, and He has.
He came and bore man's sin on the cross and
paid the penalty with His own blood. Anointed
Savior, we pour out our souls with gratitude to
Thee.

THE MEDIATOR

*For there is one God, and one mediator
between God and men, the man Christ Jesus.*
1 TIMOTHY 2:5

God is One, and there is but one Mediator
between God and man, and that is a Man; but
that Man is Christ Jesus. He is the Mediator of
the New Testament, for by means of death for the
redemption of men, He alone is qualified to act
in man's behalf.

THE MAN CHRIST JESUS

*For there is one God, and one mediator
between God and men, the man Christ Jesus.*
1 TIMOTHY 2:5

In these days when He is being demeaned by
so many who are robbing Him of His deity,
we should rejoice in the privilege offered us
of magnifying Him as both Man and God. O
Thou crucified, risen God-Man, we adore Thee.
Guide us today in our worship and work for
Thee.

GOD MANIFEST IN THE FLESH

Great is the mystery of godliness:
God was manifest in the flesh, justified in the Spirit,
seen of angels, preached unto the Gentiles, believed
on in the world, received up into glory.

1 TIMOTHY 3:16

With hearts beating in adoration, we should worship Him as the Holy Spirit of God emphasizes to us this great truth: He came, He died, He lives in us, and He lives in the glory, and we will dwell forever with Him.

BLESSED AND ONLY POTENTATE

*Our Lord Jesus Christ. . .is the blessed and only
Potentate, the King of kings, and Lord of lords.*
1 TIMOTHY 6:14–15

Limitless power is His. It is to be manifested at
His appearing who is King of kings and Lord
of lords. Our Lord will reveal Himself and will
bring with Him the crowns for the victors who
have waged a good warfare and stand ready to
receive the promised prize.

THE JUDGE OF QUICK AND DEAD

I charge thee therefore before God, and the Lord Jesus Christ, who shall judge the quick and the dead. . . . Preach the word.

2 TIMOTHY 4:1–2

We must all appear before Him to give an account for the deeds done in the body. Every man's work will be tried by fire. No one can change the record—neither God nor man. Are you ready?

THE RIGHTEOUS JUDGE

*Henceforth there is laid up for me a crown
of righteousness, which the Lord, the righteous
judge, shall give me at that day.*
2 TIMOTHY 4:8

The Lord will Himself put the crown upon the
heads of those who are true to His promises
and who look for Him. Salvation is a gift, but
crowns are for those whose lives have been lived
in obedience to the Word of God.

THE GREAT GOD

Looking for that blessed hope,
and the glorious appearing of the great
God and our Saviour Jesus Christ.

TITUS 2:13

Everywhere it is stated in the scripture that we are to look for our Lord. He will come with His glorified body. The same voice that said, "Behold my hands and my feet" (Luke 24:39) and "It is I; be not afraid" (John 6:20), will welcome us when we meet Him in the air.

GOD OUR SAVIOR

*But after that the kindness and love of
God our Saviour toward man appeared.*
TITUS 3:4

Jesus said, "I and my Father are one" (John
10:30), and He is our Savior. By our God-given
right we have been regenerated and renewed by
the Holy Spirit and should exercise our rights as
His children. Let us open wide the door of our
hearts to Thee, our God and Savior, and give
Thee the right of way today.

HEIR OF ALL THINGS

*[God] hath in these last days spoken unto us by his Son,
whom he hath appointed heir of all things,
by whom also he made the worlds.*
HEBREWS 1:2

To our Lord is ascribed glory because He is the
Creator of all things. We belong to the "Heir of
All Things." Our needs will be supplied, then,
for we are heirs of God and joint-heirs with
Jesus Christ.

THE BRIGHTNESS OF HIS GLORY

Who being the brightness of his glory. . .
HEBREWS 1:3

Do you want to visualize the glory of God?
Then gaze upon Jesus Christ. When we see
Him, we see God. How fascinating is this Bible
of ours in which we have such a revelation of
God as manifest in the flesh! With your Bible
in hand, meditate upon this revelation of Jesus
Christ and rejoice in Him as your own Lord.

II

OCTOBER

THE EXPRESS IMAGE OF HIS PERSON

Who being the brightness of his glory,
and the express image of his person. . .
HEBREWS 1:3

We have seen the Father, for we have seen the Son, a Man among men, eating, drinking, living, working with them. When we see Jesus, we see the God-Man—a perfect representation of God. Hold that truth and meditate upon it for a while, and let the Holy Spirit magnify Christ to you.

THE UPHOLDER
OF ALL THINGS

*Who being the brightness of his glory,
and the express image of his person, and upholding
all things by the word of his power...*
HEBREWS 1:3

When Jesus was broken on the cross, all of the richness of the glory of God was manifested. He is the "Upholder of All Things." He purged all sin. In the hollow of His hand are all things. You can trust all to Him.

THE SIN PURGER

*Who. . .when he had by himself purged our sins,
sat down on the right hand of the Majesty on high.*
HEBREWS 1:3

How lightly we think of sin. It is so common
that we fail to view it in God's light. Coming
short of the glory of God is sin. Sin has never
changed because human nature has never
changed. Christ came as the "Sin-Purger" and
opened the door to heaven.

GOD

But unto the Son he saith,
Thy throne, O God, is for ever and ever.
HEBREWS 1:8

Here we have the alpine height in titles for
our Lord, "Thy throne, O God!" When He
was born in a manger, God was there. When
He died on the cross, it was God Himself who
poured out His life. It is God the Son who holds
the scepter and rules the worlds, and we will
rule and reign with Him.

THE CAPTAIN OF OUR SALVATION

*For it became him. . .to make the captain
of their salvation perfect through sufferings.*
HEBREWS 2:10

He is the "Captain" (or "Author") of salvation.
The mode and method of perfection is
manifested by our Leader. He was tempted;
so are we. He suffered; so must we. He was
persecuted; so must we be. He paid the price;
so must we. The climax for Him and for us is
glory.

16
OCTOBER

THE SEED OF ABRAHAM

For verily he took not on him the nature of angels;
but he took on him the seed of Abraham.
HEBREWS 2:16

He came to fallen man and took upon Himself
the "Seed of Abraham" because He longed to
lift us to heights above those ever known to
angels. Our Lord, the wonder of Thy work for
us astonishes us. Help us to tell the story of Thy
love to our fellow men.

THE APOSTLE

Consider the Apostle. . .
of our profession, Christ Jesus.
HEBREWS 3:1

Jesus was an "Apostle" (or "Sent One"). He came to bring the most wonderful message ever intended for mortal ears: "God so loved the world!" Why did He so love it, and how was that love manifested? This Apostle did His work and has appointed us, who are believers, to carry it on to fallen men. This Apostle was faithful. Are we?

THE HIGH PRIEST

*Consider. . .the High Priest
of our profession, Christ Jesus.*
HEBREWS 3:1

We are called to consider Jesus Christ as "High Priest." Could we but make it our life habit to, every morning, spend a few moments in contemplation of Him as our High Priest, and take up life's duties with that picture before us, seeing Him clothed in the garments of the High Priest, we would be better believers.

THE BUILDER

*This man was counted worthy of more glory
than Moses, inasmuch as he who hath builded
the house hath more honour than the house.*

HEBREWS 3:3

Christ is here set forth as the "Builder." The
foundation of the house is laid in Him. We are
temples of the Holy Spirit now. Christ dwells
within us. Let Christ have His way in fitting us
for our appointed places in the Temple of God.

THE GREAT HIGH PRIEST

Seeing then that we have a great high priest. . .
Jesus the Son of God, let us hold fast our profession.
HEBREWS 4:14

Jesus is our "Great High Priest." We can come
with boldness to the throne of grace and will
find grace for every need. He settled every claim
against us. Satan may condemn us, but our
Great High Priest holds forth His pierced hands
and that is enough.

21
OCTOBER

A PRIEST FOREVER

Thou art a priest for ever after the order of Melchisedec.
HEBREWS 5:6

Will Christ be our representative throughout eternity? Yes—and we will be His representatives throughout eternity. For our new life is eternal. He is our eternal High Priest, and we are to be kings and priests in association with Him. We are poor, undone, hell-deserving sinners, but through Him, we are lifted to eternal heights.

AUTHOR OF
ETERNAL SALVATION

*And being made perfect, he became the author
of eternal salvation unto all them that obey him.*
HEBREWS 5:9

Christ was perfected through suffering. When
He bore our sin on the cross, the unchanging
law of God was in operation, and He suffered
separation from God. There was but one way by
which sinful men could be made righteous, and
that was by the Savior's taking our place, which
He did.

THE FORERUNNER

Whither the forerunner is for us entered, even Jesus.
HEBREWS 6:20

Our hope is an anchor, which entereth into that which is beyond the veil, and our Forerunner has entered beyond the veil into the Holy of Holies. Our hope is anchored in Him. We are a part of Him. We can never be separated from Him because He lives in us, and we shall live and be with Him forever.

KING OF RIGHTEOUSNESS

First being by interpretation King of righteousness. . .
HEBREWS 7:2

Christ is "King of Righteousness," for He is
the King of kings. All of our righteousness is
as filthy rags, but "Christ is the end of the law
for righteousness to everyone that believeth"
(Romans 10:4). We believe in Him, and it
is counted unto us for righteousness. His
righteousness is put to our account and we are
associated with the Righteous King forever.
Hallelujah!

KING OF PEACE

*After that also King of Salem,
which is, King of peace.*
HEBREWS 7:2

Righteousness is the basis of peace. The "King of Peace" dwells in us and we dwell in Him. He came and preached peace. He went to the cross and made peace possible. "Great peace have they which love thy law" (Psalm 119:165). O Thou King of Peace, may Thy peace which passeth all understanding garrison our souls this day.

THE SURETY

*By so much was Jesus made a
surety of a better testament.*
HEBREWS 7:22

Sometimes we lack confidence in the finished
work, which our Christ has wrought for us.
But we have here the statement that Christ has
become our "Surety," or Security. We are made
confident by the fact that He has placed Himself
as our Bondsman, our Security. We can draw
our drafts upon the Bank of heaven and He has
pledged Himself as our Security.

OUR INTERCESSOR

*Wherefore he is able also to save them
to the uttermost that come unto God by him,
seeing he ever liveth to make intercession for them.*
HEBREWS 7:25

He saves to the fullest extent. Satan may bring charges against us, and sometimes they may be well founded, but our "Intercessor" is there. He bore our sins, carried our sorrows, meets every accusation. What a wonderful Savior!

Separate from Sinners

For such an high priest became us,
who is. . .separate from sinners.
Hebrews 7:26

Though He was separate from sinners, He did
not avoid them as we are wont to do. No one
ever loved them as He did—the Holy One. We
must not miss this suggestion if we are to be like
Him, loving sinners and following His example.

29

OCTOBER

HIGHER THAN THE HEAVENS

For such an high priest became us,
who is. . .higher than the heavens.
HEBREWS 7:26

Someday from the dizzying heights He will descend with a shout. His voice will ring out in glad expectancy. He is coming for you and for me. Our faith in His finished work has sealed us forever to Himself. Lord, Thou exalted One, we give Thee all praise and wait with glad hearts for Thy coming.

THE MINISTER OF
THE SANCTUARY

A minister of the sanctuary, and of the true tabernacle,
which the Lord pitched, and not man.
HEBREWS 8:2

He is the King, but He is still a servant of men,
serving in our behalf, loving us, ministering to
us. Dwelling in our hearts by the Holy Spirit,
He performs every needed function in the
cleansing and preparing of His people for their
access to God.

MEDIATOR OF A BETTER COVENANT

But now. . .he is the mediator of a better covenant.
HEBREWS 8:6

He promises to put His laws into our minds and write them on our hearts and says, "I will be their God and they shall be my people. . . . I will forgive their iniquity, and their sin will I remember no more" (Jeremiah 31:33–34 ASV). Let us remember, then, that we are His temple, and He will perfect His work in and through us.

THE TESTATOR

*For where a testament is, there must also
of necessity be the death of the testator.*
HEBREWS 9:16

A testator is a man who makes and leaves a
will, or testament, at death. Christ has left a
testament and a will. He died for us. He shed
His blood as a freewill offering in our behalf.
The sin question is settled forever for us who
believe in Jesus Christ, our "Testator."

HE THAT SHALL COME

For yet a little while, and he that shall
come will come, and will not tarry.
HEBREWS 10:37

The Christian life is built not only on the
present but on the unseen future. God has never
broken a promise and He never can. Nothing
pleases our Lord more than implicit faith in His
Word and work. Lord, we are looking for Thy
coming in the clouds of glory. Come quickly!

NOVEMBER 3

A REWARDER

*But without faith it is impossible to please him:
for he that cometh to God must believe that he is, and
that he is a rewarder of them that diligently seek him.*

HEBREWS 11:6

Our Lord Jesus Christ is the Judge. He
pronounces the sentence. He gives the reward.
What we do we must do in His name and for
His glory. We must live for Him and be willing
to die for Him. Our reward awaits us.

THE AUTHOR OF FAITH

Looking unto Jesus the author. . .of our faith.
HEBREWS 12:2

The "Author (Leader) of our Faith" is Jesus.
Look to Him, for the inspiration to faith is
found in Him. He inspires us by His sacrificial
death and by His precious promises. O Thou
great Author of our Faith, keep our eyes on
Thee, and with unwavering faith may we follow
Thee to the end.

THE FINISHER OF FAITH

Looking unto Jesus the. . .finisher of our faith.
HEBREWS 12:2

He is the "Finisher of Our Faith." Our Lord set us the example of faith, and He will perfect it in us. There will be trials, but we are to "count it all joy." He did, and step by step He leads us on. The best is always before us, though the last link may be the cross—but then "face-to-face with him"!

MEDIATOR OF
THE NEW COVENANT

To Jesus the mediator of the new covenant,
and to the blood of sprinkling, that speaketh
better things than that of Abel.
HEBREWS 12:24

Let our eyes rest upon the cross. Let us see the
blood. Let it separate us from a sinful world
and make of us witnesses to its cleansing power.
Lord, give us the needed grace to witness to
the efficacy of the atoning blood of the New
Covenant.

MY HELPER

So that we may boldly say,
The Lord is my helper.
HEBREWS 13:6

Courage of conviction is the crying need of
the Christian today—conviction based on
God's Holy Word. "He hath said, I will never
leave thee nor forsake thee" (Hebrews 13:5).
Faith takes hold upon this promise and allows
nothing to move it. Lord Jesus, our Helper, help
us to lean hard upon Thy gracious promises and
have a joyful life today.

JESUS CHRIST THE SAME

*Jesus Christ the same yesterday,
and to day, and for ever.*
HEBREWS 13:8

The world is a sinful, restless place. Uncertainty is written everywhere in human life, but the Living Word and the Written Word are unchangeable. Lord Jesus Christ, Thou art the same. Help us to sense it and intensify our love for Thee, and may it also be always "the same."

9
NOVEMBER

THE GREAT SHEPHERD
OF THE SHEEP

Our Lord Jesus, that great shepherd of the sheep.
HEBREWS 13:20

He is here pictured as the "Great Shepherd,"
raised from the dead, sanctified by the blood of
the everlasting covenant, which is able to make
us "perfect in every good work to do his will"
(Hebrews 13:21). How? By working in us and
through us that which pleases Himself.

THAT WORTHY NAME

*Do not they blaspheme that worthy
name by the which ye are called?*
JAMES 2:7

The emphasis is on the "Worthy Name."
That Name is sacred, "for there is none other
name. . .whereby we must be saved" (Acts 4:12).
In that Name we approach our Father. Lord
Jesus, we come in Thy Worthy Name and ask
for forgiveness for our sins of neglect and ask for
Thy power for service this day.

A CHIEF CORNERSTONE

Behold, I lay in Sion a chief corner stone. . .
and he that believeth on him shall not be confounded.
1 PETER 2:6

Christ is the "Chief Cornerstone" of the most wonderful temple ever conceived. This temple is built of human lives—blood-washed saints of the Living God. It is the dwelling place of God. From the dome the chimes ring out the call, "Exalt the Lord our God and worship at His feet."

A LAMB WITHOUT BLEMISH OR SPOT

But with the precious blood of Christ,
as of a lamb without blemish and without spot.
1 PETER 1:19

Here we have two words so marvelously wonderful that we are hesitant in our effort to make any comment—"Blood" and "Lamb." The spotless, pure Lamb of God finished the work of redemption. Is He precious to us? So precious that we would be willing to die in His behalf?

A LIVING STONE

*To whom coming, as unto a living stone, disallowed
indeed of men, but chosen of God, and precious.*
1 PETER 2:4

He is living. He lives in the lives of the
redeemed. He is the chosen of God. He is the
Stone cut out of the mountain. He is the One in
whom and through whom we have everlasting
life. He will live through eternity and we will
live in and with Him.

AN ELECT STONE

Behold, I lay in Sion a chief corner stone, elect. . . .
1 PETER 2:6

The "Elect Stone" is the Chief Cornerstone
of the temple of God, which is composed of
believers who were chosen before the foundation
of the world. We were chosen in Him, and He
was chosen in the council chamber of heaven to
become the Elect Stone—the One who should
be the Head of the Corner.

A PRECIOUS STONE

Behold, I lay in Sion a chief corner stone. . .precious.
1 PETER 2:6

The more we know about Him, the more
wonderful He becomes; and the more intimately
we know Him, the more precious He is. He so
loved you and me that He laid aside His royal
robe, arrayed Himself in human flesh, and then
poured out His precious blood for us. Should
He not be precious to us?

A STONE OF STUMBLING

*The stone which the builders disallowed. . .
is made. . .a stone of stumbling.*
1 PETER 2:7–8

To those who willfully reject Him and stumble
into the abyss, there are weeping and wailing.
To those who pride themselves upon their
education, wealth, or position, and refuse to
bow at His feet, He is a "Stone of Stumbling."
How subtle is Satan! How hard is the human
heart!

A ROCK OF OFFENSE

*The stone which the builders disallowed. . .
is made. . .a rock of offence.*
1 PETER 2:7–8

The Jewish nation is an illustration of our
theme. Every possible effort was made by
Christ to win His own people to Himself.
But they would not have Him. What a blow
has fallen upon them! How can it be that our
loving, crucified Lord should become to so
many a "Rock of Offense" instead of the "Chief
Cornerstone"?

THE BISHOP OF SOULS

For ye were as sheep going astray; but are now returned unto the Shepherd and Bishop of your souls.
1 PETER 2:25

He is the "Bishop." He is the imparter of life. His eye is upon us. He is the One whose heart goes out in love to the lost, straying sheep and who never fails in His own good way and time to bring them back to the fold (the true church).

THE JUST

For Christ also hath once suffered for sins,
the just for the unjust.
1 PETER 3:18

How strong is the contrast here—the Just for
the unjust! Why this sacrifice? That He might
bring us to God, making it possible for us to
have access through the rent veil to the Holy of
Holies. He was the Just, the Sinless One. Jesus
kept the law and took our place, setting us free
from the penalty.

THE CHIEF SHEPHERD

*When the chief Shepherd shall appear, ye shall
receive a crown of glory that fadeth not away.*
1 PETER 5:4

We visualize Him with shepherd staff leading
His sheep and enfolding them in safety. But
there is the glad day to come when He will
crown His loyal ones. Is there anything more
to be desired than the privilege accorded us of
making Him now the chiefest of ten thousand
in our hearts?

THE DAY STAR

*We have also a more sure word of prophecy;
whereunto ye do well that ye take heed. . .
until. . .the day star arise in your hearts.*
2 PETER 1:19

Our hearts are darkened by the evil nature
within us, but when Jesus comes into our
hearts, He illumines the Word of God and
shines with all the effulgence of His glory.
Perpetual day is for those who walk in His
light.

22
NOVEMBER

LORD AND SAVIOR JESUS CHRIST

But grow in grace, and in the knowledge
of our Lord and Saviour Jesus Christ.
2 PETER 3:18

Growing into Him is a part of eternal life.
How shall we obey this command? Study His
Word. It is the Lamp and Light. Search this
Word. It is a mine of treasures. Submit to the
commandments of the Word. Then will we be
wise indeed.

THE WORD OF LIFE

That which was from the beginning, which. . .
our hands have handled, of the Word of life.
1 JOHN 1:1

Here we have John saying concerning Him
who was God that he had looked upon Him
and handled Him. He is the life-giving Word.
The need of a lost world is to know Him. The
business of believers is to tell the wonderful
story. Paint the picture. Live the life. Sow the
seed.

THAT ETERNAL LIFE

*That eternal life, which was with the Father,
and was manifested unto us.*

1 JOHN 1:2

He is "Eternal Life." He has imparted eternal life to us through the channel of faith, and the indwelling Holy Spirit certifies to it. Nothing can ever separate us from the love of God which is in Christ Jesus our Lord. We are God's rich children. Our treasures are for evermore.

THE ADVOCATE

*My little children, these things write I unto you,
that ye sin not. And if any man sin, we have an
advocate with the Father, Jesus Christ the righteous.*

1 JOHN 2:1

When Satan charges us with sin, Christ
represents us and defends us. He is the attorney
who handles our case. His propitiation (or
covering for sin) is manifested in all His work
for us.

JESUS CHRIST THE RIGHTEOUS

*If any man sin, we have an advocate with
the Father, Jesus Christ the righteous.*
1 JOHN 2:1

Jesus Christ is the "Righteous One." No
unrighteous man could be our Advocate or
Judge. He must Himself be just, and He is also
the Justifier. What a consolation to us as poor
sinners to know that we are justified from all
things from which we could not be justified by
the law of Moses.

27
NOVEMBER

THE PROPITIATION

And he is the propitiation for our sins: and not for ours only, but also for the sins of the whole world.
1 JOHN 2:2

God's wrath against sin must be appeased, and the provision for that satisfaction is in His Son. Wonderful love of God, the One who makes the fact of propitiation clear to us through the Word! How is the "whole world" to know this truth? Someone must go. Will we go?

28
NOVEMBER

THE SON

*And we have seen and do testify that the Father
sent the Son to be the Saviour of the world.*

1 JOHN 4:14

The Son was sent for one specific purpose—to
be the Savior of lost men. The business of the
believer is to testify to that fact. It is not a
question of church membership or of worldly
possessions, but of knowledge of Him. Do you
know Him? Then go and testify of Him.

The Savior of the World

*And we have seen and do testify that the Father
sent the Son to be the Saviour of the world.*
1 John 4:14

A lost and ruined world, bound by the shackles
of sin, dominated by the demon Satan, helpless
and hopeless! What can be done? Only God
can solve the question, and He has. He sent His
Son. He has saved us. We must testify.

THE TRUE GOD

We know that the Son of God is come, and hath given us an understanding, that we may know him that is true, and we are in him that is true, even in his Son Jesus Christ. This is the true God, and eternal life.

1 JOHN 5:20

There is but one God. We praise God—the "True God"—that we are in Him and He in us. Nothing can ever separate us.

ETERNAL LIFE

This is the true God, and eternal life.
1 JOHN 5:20

To believers, eternity means life with God
our Savior, and we look forward with joyful
anticipation; but to the unsaved, it is a fearful
prospect. Lord, help us in dealing with people to
be truthful and loving as we paint the pictures
of a future without a Savior.

THE SON OF THE FATHER

*Grace be with you, mercy, and peace,
from God the Father, and from the Lord Jesus Christ,
the Son of the Father, in truth and love.*

2 JOHN 3

Truth without love may be cold, harsh. Love
without truth may be purely sentimental,
but when combined, they truly represent the
message of the "Son of the Father," for the Son
is the Truth, manifested in Love.

3
DECEMBER

JESUS CHRIST

Grace be unto you, and peace, from him which is, and which was, and which is to come; and from the seven Spirits which are before his throne; and from Jesus Christ, who is the faithful witness, and the first begotten of the dead, and the prince of the kings of the earth.

REVELATION 1:4–5

O Thou anointed Savior, help us to unite with all the heavenly host in glorifying Thy name.

THE FAITHFUL WITNESS

Jesus Christ, who is the faithful witness.
REVELATION 1:5

This was His mission—to bear faithful witness.
The unsaved are waiting for the testimony by
lip and life of professing Christians, and as they
behold it, they are convicted by the Holy Spirit.
May the Holy Spirit Himself so control our lives
that we shall count it our highest privilege to
manifest Him before a gainsaying world.

THE FIRST BEGOTTEN
OF THE DEAD

Jesus Christ, who is. . .the first begotten of the dead.
REVELATION 1:5

Jesus Christ raised Lazarus from the dead, but
He Himself came forth from the grave by His
own power. He is the forerunner of the saints
who shall also be raised from the dead. Our
Lord, we look and long for Thy coming in Thy
glorified body that we may be with Thee and
like Thee.

THE PRINCE OF THE KINGS OF THE EARTH

Jesus Christ, who is. . .the prince of the kings of the earth.
REVELATION 1:5

He is Lord of all who exercise authority and King of all who reign. He has not yet asserted His authoritative rights. They are still in abeyance, but the day is coming when every scepter will be broken and every crown laid at His feet.

7

DECEMBER

THE ALPHA AND OMEGA

*I am Alpha and Omega, the beginning and the
ending, saith the Lord, which is, and which was,
and which is to come, the Almighty.*
REVELATION 1:8

"Alpha" is the first letter of the Greek alphabet,
and "Omega" is the last. So our Lord is First
and Last. He is the Source of all truth, of all the
promises given in the Word of God, of all the
prophecies, and of all commands.

8

DECEMBER

THE ALMIGHTY

I am. . .the Almighty.
REVELATION 1:8

Our Lord Jesus Christ is the All-Sufficient One.
Listen to His voice—the "I Am" speaking to
us. His voice and message demand attention
and obedience. We can trust Him and trust His
message. Nothing can fail of all that He says.
The Bible is an infallible book. Its message is an
infallible message. What an abiding place for us
who are His dear children!

THE FIRST AND THE LAST

And he laid his right hand upon me, saying unto me,
Fear not; I am the first and the last.
REVELATION 1:17

He was the First-Begotten. He puts His right
hand on us and says in tenderest tones, "Fear
not." He draws us to Himself and says, "Pillow
your head upon My shoulder. Have no fear.
You are Mine. I purchased you at a great price.
Perfect love casts out fear."

10
DECEMBER

HE THAT LIVETH

I am he that liveth, and was dead; and, behold,
I am alive for evermore, Amen.
REVELATION 1:18

He ever liveth to make intercession for us. In love for us and through grace He died for us. He holds the keys of death and hell. The sting of death is sin and the strength of sin is the law, but thanks be to God who giveth us the victory through our Lord Jesus Christ!

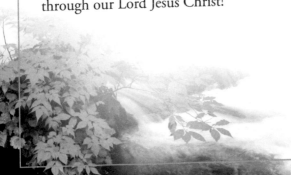

THE HIDDEN MANNA

To him that overcometh
will I give to eat of the hidden manna.
REVELATION 2:17

What is this "Hidden Manna?" Is it not Himself
who is the Bread of Life? The voice of the
Holy Spirit is heard speaking to the churches a
message for the overcomers. From the glory land
our Lord feeds His flock with the Word of God.
We who feed upon Him shall live forever.

THE MORNING STAR

And I will give him the morning star.
REVELATION 2:28

He will give us Himself, for He is the "Morning
Star." It is night now for this poor old world.
It grows darker and darker, but our eyes are
heavenward. As the "Sun of Righteousness" to
Israel, He brought them blessings; but before
the glad day for Israel comes, the Morning Star
must shine, and a ray of light will appear for His
own heavenly ones.

THE AMEN

These things saith the Amen.
REVELATION 3:14

The "Amen" here is our Lord—the Faithful
Witness. He has said "Amen" to every truth
of the scripture, but the church has failed to
follow in His footsteps. She says, "I am rich
and increased with goods and have need of
nothing." She has been neither cold nor hot,
but a lukewarm product. God pity her! To what
extent are we responsible? God forgive us.

THE FAITHFUL
AND TRUE WITNESS

These things saith. . .the faithful and true witness.
REVELATION 3:14

He is the "Faithful and True Witness." Have we
been faithful and true witnesses? Alas, we must
bow our heads with shame as we remember our
failure. Will we be faithful? O Lord our Savior,
forgive us for our faithlessness as witnesses.
Anoint us to stand before a lost world and be
true at any cost.

THE BEGINNING OF THE CREATION OF GOD

These things saith. . .the beginning of the creation of God.
REVELATION 3:14

There are four headships ascribed to our Lord Jesus Christ. First—of the body. Second—of the race. Third—of the creation. Fourth—of every man. Let us seek earnestly to recognize the might and power and authority of our Lord who left heaven and laid down His life for us.

THE LION OF
THE TRIBE OF JUDAH

*Behold, the Lion of the tribe of Judah. . .hath prevailed
to open the book, and to loose the seven seals thereof.*
REVELATION 5:5

The characteristics of a lion are manifest in the
life and work of the Messiah. He will arrest
every opposing force of Satan and establish His
universal kingdom. Glory be to God, we will be
with Him and like Him in the final overthrow
of Satan's kingdom.

THE ROOT OF DAVID

Weep not: behold, the Lion of the tribe of Judah,
the Root of David, hath prevailed.
REVELATION 5:5

Jesus was the "Root" that was to rise and
reign over the Gentiles, and in Him would
the Gentiles trust. He was worthy to open the
book because He was slain. What wonders
confront us concerning Him! Lord, we marvel
more and more that Thou couldst ever love us
and die for us.

HOLY AND TRUE

*How long, O Lord, holy and true, dost thou not judge
and avenge our blood on them that dwell on the earth?*
REVELATION 6:10

This is the heart cry of those who suffered death
for Jesus' sake because they were true to Him
in life and testimony. Is it not such a cry as
sometimes bursts forth from our own souls as
we see the hatred of Satan for the souls of men?
We must abide in faith.

THE LAMB IN THE MIDST OF THE THRONE

For the Lamb which is in the midst of the throne shall feed them, and shall lead them unto living fountains of waters: and God shall wipe away all tears from their eyes.
REVELATION 7:17

Here is a wonderful picture of our future dwelling place. He that sitteth upon the throne will dwell amongst us. He Himself shall feed us, and we shall drink from the living fountains.

THE LAMB SLAIN

All that dwell upon the earth shall worship him,
whose names are not written in the book of life of
the Lamb slain from the foundation of the world.

REVELATION 13:8

Jesus was ordained from the foundation of the
world to suffer upon the cross for our sins. The
only means of salvation for men has been the
shedding of His blood. What a place in our
hearts the Lamb of God should have!

21
DECEMBER

KING OF SAINTS

Just and true are thy ways, thou King of saints.
REVELATION 15:3

This title is better rendered "King of Nations" or "King of the Ages." What a picture is here! A judgment is awaiting the nations. Seven angels with the seven last plagues are there. There are the harps of God and the song of Moses. The song is of victory over the beast and his image. What a day!

LORD OF LORDS

He is Lord of lords, and King of kings: and they that are with him are called, and chosen, and faithful.
REVELATION 17:14

The world has been the sphere of the conflict of the ages, but there is coming a day when that war will cease, and that is the day which is portrayed in this verse. All of the kings must bow to Him. We look forward to the victory which is prophesied.

KING OF KINGS

The Lamb shall overcome them:
for he is. . .King of kings.
REVELATION 17:14

He has upon His garments and upon His thigh
the name "King of kings." The power of God's
Word is irresistible. How foolish are they whose
feeble hands are raised up against the King of
kings—the Mighty One! What judgment awaits
all those who oppose Him and His unerring
Word.

LORD GOD OMNIPOTENT

*I heard as it were the voice of a great multitude. . .saying,
Alleluia: for the Lord God omnipotent reigneth.*
REVELATION 19:6

What words can compare with the words of
God which are associated with this matchless
scene. He is coming, the Omnipotent One—
and we will be with Him. Alleluia! O Thou
Mighty One, gird us with Thy strength that we
may do our best to hasten that glad day.

FAITHFUL AND TRUE

And he that sat upon [the horse]
was called Faithful and True.
REVELATION 19:11

To no one else could that title be applied but
the Lord Jesus. He was faithful to the truth
always and faithful in its application, whether
in promises of blessings or cursing. There is
no change in Him, the Living Word, and not
one jot or tittle can be changed in the Written
Word.

THE WORD OF GOD

He was clothed with a vesture dipped in blood:
and his name is called The Word of God.

REVELATION 19:13

We have seen Him by faith. Clothed in a
blood-dipped vesture, He leads the armies of
heaven, including all the saints of the Old and
New Testament, to victory. Pity those whose
eyes have been closed to the vision of the
real Christ and who only have a sentimental
conception of Him.

THE TEMPLE

*I saw no temple therein: for the Lord God Almighty
and the Lamb are the temple of it.*
REVELATION 21:22

He is the Temple! Whatever significance there
may be in the dimensions and the structure—
whether literal or pictorial—it means "great
in size; rich in adornment." We stand in awe,
but—glory be to God—we anticipate with
increasing joy the vision which awaits us and its
full realization.

The Light of the City

And the Lamb is the light thereof.
REVELATION 21:23

The Lamb is the "Light of the World" and He is also the Light of the Eternal City. There is no need of sun or moon, for He who created all things hath provided a Light for the City and it is the glory of His own countenance. In this Light, kings and people will pay their tribute.

THE OFFSPRING OF DAVID

*I am the root and the offspring of David,
and the bright and morning star.*
REVELATION 22:16

God the Son created the heavens and the earth
and all that are therein, yet He is the "Offspring
of David," David's Lord, and David's Son. He
was born King of the Jews and died King of the
Jews and someday He will reign King of the
Jews.

THE BRIGHT
AND MORNING STAR

*I Jesus have sent mine angel to testify unto
you these things in the churches. I am. . .
the bright and morning star.*

REVELATION 22:16

Before the millennium dawns, He will be to the
church the "Bright and Morning Star." He will
dispel the darkness for us before the prophesied
judgments come upon a weary, sin-sick world;
and before the glories depicted in this chapter
are revealed, He will appear as the Bright and
Morning Star.

THE TESTIFIER

He which testifieth these things saith, Surely I come quickly. Amen. Even so, come, Lord Jesus.
REVELATION 22:20

The days grow darker for the church and for the world. We are thinking of those whose future is to be full of woe and anguish. The "Testifier" entreats us to testify to the lost. Let us point them to the Lamb of God and plead with sinners to accept Him and with the saints to look for Him.

INDEX